# Say & Glue® Phonological Awareness
## Fun Sheets

Written by Alyson D. Price, M.S.P., CCC-SLP
and Jane B. Senn, M.S.P., CCC-SLP

Edited by Wendy C. Ward, M.A.T. and Thomas Webber

www.superduperinc.com
1-800-277-8737

ISBN 1-978-58650-631-5

# Dedication

We would like to dedicate this book to all of the students who have taught us the importance of strong phonological awareness skills and the significant role these skills play in the development of speech and language and in learning to read and write. Through your daily hard work, you have taught us more than you could ever know. "Thank you" Caleb, Dustin H., Dustin R., Evan, Jared, Jeriod, Joseph, Josh, Kieyon, and Lee!

We would like to express our deep appreciation to our very special husbands and children. We could never thank you enough for the love and support you have freely given to us throughout the years. Much love to Jeff, Brittany, and Austin from Alyson, and to Randy, Kyle, and Amanda from Jane. We would also like to express our sincere gratitude to our mothers, fathers, sisters, and brothers for their lifelong unconditional love and support. Our dear families, all of you will always be the most important people in our lives.

We would also like to express our appreciation to the *South Carolina Speech-Language-Hearing Association* for supporting the work of public school speech-language pathologists and therapists in the effort to address literacy. The association recognizes the important role speech-language pathologists and therapists play in serving students who exhibit problems with phonological awareness skills. Sponsoring continuing education workshops throughout the state and at the annual association convention has helped to improve awareness and professional skills. As a result, many students of South Carolina have benefited and have become better at reading, writing, and communicating.

# Introduction

We are seeing an increase in the number of both preschool and elementary aged children in our caseloads that have difficulty in the area of phonological awareness. Many children in speech and language therapy have difficulty with some of the early preliteracy skills, which interferes with their ability to learn to read.

A child's knowledge of the sounds of language normally progresses from very simple discrimination of sounds to a more complex level, which is termed phonological awareness. This level includes the ability to blend, segment, count, and/or manipulate sounds into various combinations that make up the words of our English language. Most recent research suggests that children have at least some awareness of word sounds and how words link into sentences prior to kindergarten. By age six, the majority of children should be able to count the sound parts in a word.

The last few years, we have noticed that many children we are seeing for speech and language therapy exhibit weak phonological awareness skills. Many of the elementary aged students have not mastered these important preliteracy skills needed to be a successful reader. We have also discovered that preschoolers, as young as age three, can be taught these skills by spending just a few minutes of each session targeting phonological awareness.

While working on these skills, we have not been able to find a program that offers all of the various levels of phonological awareness in a fun, motivating method for the students. Most of the therapy we have done has either been pulled from various other sources or created by the therapist. Therefore, we decided to develop a book that covers many levels of phonological awareness using fun, motivating activities that the students would enjoy. *Say & Glue® for Phonological Awareness* covers all of the significant phonological awareness skills that children need to develop a solid foundation for good reading.

# About This Book

## Rhyming with Nonsense Words

This section includes various picture scenes with six pictures related to the scene on the bottom for gluing. The SLP/teacher says a nonsense word, and the child finds the picture that rhymes with it to glue on the scene. For example, a picture of a farm scene has a picture of a *horse*. The SLP/teacher says, "Find a picture that rhymes with *norse*." The child finds the picture of the *horse* and glues it on the scene (p. 3).

## Rhyming Sentences

This section consists of four sentences with a picture clue and eight small pictures at the bottom to color and cut out. The sentences have two blanks to glue in the missing words. The SLP/teacher reads a target word for each sentence, and the child finds the two pictures that rhyme with the target word. For example, a picture clue has a boy with a calf who has eaten half of his pie. The SLP/teacher says, "Find the pictures that rhyme with *laugh*." The child would find the *calf* and *half*. Then, looking at the picture clue, glue the picture so the sentence would read "The boy had to laugh when his calf ate half of his pie" (p. 14).

## Fill in the Rhyming Word

This section consists of ten picture scenes with six pictures related to the scene on the bottom for gluing and six sentence clues. The SLP/teacher reads the sentence clue, leaving off the last word, and the child finds the picture that rhymes and glues it on the picture scene. For example, a picture of a street scene includes a store picture for gluing. The SLP/teacher reads the sentence clue "When I go in, I always want <u>more</u>. It's fun to look around in the toy _____." The child finds the picture of the *store* and glues it on the picture (p. 26).

## Which Rhyming Word Belongs?

This section consists of five pairs of rhyming picture words and an empty space for gluing a third one. Five pictures for gluing are also on the bottom. The SLP/teacher reads the two rhyming words, and the child finds the picture that rhymes and glues it in the empty space. For example, the SLP/teacher would read the rhyming words *stop* and *top*. The child finds the picture of the *mop* and glues it in the empty space. There are five pages of one-syllable words and five pages of two-syllable words (p. 38).

#BK-330 Say & Glue® Phonological Awareness • ©2006 Super Duper® Publications • 1-800-277-8737 • www.superduperinc.com

# Blending Words

This section includes two levels of skills. Various picture scenes have six pictures related to the scene at the bottom for gluing. In the first level, the SLP/teacher says a two or three syllable word, which is broken into syllables. The child finds the picture of the word and glues it on the page. For example, a picture scene of a party would have a picture of a cupcake. The SLP/teacher says, "*Cup-cake.* Find the word that I just said, and glue it on the page." The child finds the picture of the cupcake and glues it on. In the second level, the SLP/teacher names one of the pictures breaking the word into phonemes. The child finds the picture and glues it on the page. For example, in a rainy day picture scene, the SLP/teacher says, "*F-i-sh.* Find the word that I just said, and glue it on the page." The child finds the picture of the fish and glues it on the page (p. 60).

# Segmentation

This section includes various pages with twelve pictures at the bottom of the page for gluing. The SLP/teacher says a compound word, and the child has to find the two small words that make up the big word and glue them on the page. For example, the SLP/teacher says, "Listen to this word, *rainbow*. Find the two small words that make up that word, and glue them on the page." The child finds the pictures of the *rain* and *bow* and glues them on the page (p. 62).

# Syllable Counting

This section includes a page divided in half with a number on each side. Pictures for gluing are at the bottom. The child names each picture, decides on the number of syllables, or parts of the word, and glues it on the half of the page with that number. For example, a page has the numbers two and three on it. The child selects the picture of *apple*. After saying the word, he determines that it has two syllables and glues it on the half of the page with the number two (p. 70).

# Letter Sounds

This area has three sections. In the first section, a page is divided into fourths with a letter in each area. Pictures at the bottom of the page start with one of the four letters on the page. The child glues the pictures in the section with the letter that each picture begins with. For example, the picture of a *pear* would be glued on the fourth of the page with the letter *P* (p. 78). The second section is the same as the first except the sound is on the <u>end</u> of the word instead of the beginning.

The third section contains pictures of people with names. The pictures at the bottom of the page are glued with the person whose name starts the same as the picture. For example, a page has pictures of someone named *Paula*, *Mary*, and *David*. Pictures at the bottom include *pearls*, *mouse,* and *doll*. The *pearls* will be glued with *Paula*, the *mouse* with *Mary*, and the *doll* with *David* (p. 89).

## Syllable/Phoneme Deletion

This section includes various picture scenes with six pictures related to the scene at the bottom for gluing. The SLP/teacher says a compound word and asks the child to repeat the word, deleting a syllable. The child finds the picture of the target word and glues it on the page. For example, a home scene would have a picture of a dog. The SLP/teacher says, "Say *doghouse*. Now it without *house*. What new word did you say? Find that picture (dog), and glue it on your page." (p. 96).

Another level included in this section deletes a syllable or phoneme; however, the word is <u>not</u> a compound word. For example, the SLP/teacher says, "Find the *pedal*. Say *pedal*. Now say it without *dal*. The child follows the instructions, then finds the pedal and glues the picture on the page (p. 101).

## Syllable/Phoneme Addition

This section includes various picture scenes with six pictures related to the scene at the bottom for gluing. The SLP/teacher says a real or nonsense word and asks the child to repeat the word adding a syllable or phoneme. The child finds the picture of the new word and glues it on the page. For example, a picture scene of a diner would have a picture of a milkshake. The SLP/teacher says, "Say *milk*. Now say it with *shake* at the end. What new word did you say? Find that picture and glue it on your page." (p. 106). Another example is in a picture scene of a movie that includes a picture of salt. The SLP/teacher says, "Say *sal*. Now say it with *ty* at the end. What new word did you say? Find that picture, and glue it on the page." (p. 111).

## Manipulation of Phonemes

This section includes various pages with directions for manipulating the phonemes in words. The bottom of the page has pictures of the new words that the child makes by manipulating the sounds. The SLP/teacher reads the directions. The child follows the directions and says the new word. Then, the child finds the picture that matches the new word and tapes/glues it on the box next to the sentence.

#BK-330 Say & Glue® Phonological Awareness • ©2006 Super Duper® Publications • 1-800-277-8737 • www.superduperinc.com

# Table of Contents

# Table of Contents

# Parent/Helper Letter

Date:_____


Dear Parent/Helper,

Your child is currently working on improving his/her phonological awareness skills. These skills are extremely important for future success in reading.

The attached activity will help your child develop skills in the area of:

- ❏ Discrimination of Rhyming Words
- ❏ Production of Rhyming Words
- ❏ Blending Syllables
- ❏ Segmentation of Syllables
- ❏ Identification of Phonemes
- ❏ Syllable/Phoneme Addition
- ❏ Syllable/Phoneme Deletion
- ❏ Manipulation of Phonemes


This activity does not require much time to complete. It requires your child to <u>listen</u> <u>carefully</u> to the words or sounds you say to them.

Have fun improving your child's phonological awareness skills!


_____
Name

# Phonological Awareness Criterion Test

Name:_____ Age: _____ Grade: _____

PreTest Date: _____ PostTest Date: _____ Test Administrator: _____

## Rhyming

**Identification**
*Listen. I am going to say two words.*
*Tell me if these words rhyme.*

|  | Pre | Post |
|---|---|---|
| car - jar | _____ | _____ |
| ring - wing | _____ | _____ |
| bat - bar | _____ | _____ |
| rose - nose | _____ | _____ |
| see - sat | _____ | _____ |

Percent Correct    ⬜/5 %    ⬜/5 %

**Production**
*Listen. I am going to say a word.*
*Tell me a word that rhymes with the word I said.*

|  | Pre | Post |
|---|---|---|
| sky | _____ | _____ |
| hay | _____ | _____ |
| sue | _____ | _____ |
| boy | _____ | _____ |
| hot | _____ | _____ |

Percent Correct    ⬜/5 %    ⬜/5 %

## Blending

*Listen to the word parts <u>el-e-phant</u> (say the word parts <u>slowly</u>). They make the word <u>elephant</u>. Tell me what word these word parts make. (For this section, add the two columns together to calculate a percentage correct.)*

|  | Pre | Post |
|---|---|---|
| hot - dog | _____ | _____ |
| tooth - brush | _____ | _____ |
| air - plane | _____ | _____ |
| door - bell | _____ | _____ |
| horse - shoe | _____ | _____ |

|  | Pre | Post |
|---|---|---|
| yel - low | _____ | _____ |
| cir - cus | _____ | _____ |
| e - ra - ser | _____ | _____ |
| tel - e - phone | _____ | _____ |
| mag - a - zine | _____ | _____ |

Percent Correct    ⬜/10 %    ⬜/10 %

## Segmentation

*Say each word slowly so I can hear its parts,*
*like <u>ba-by</u> (say the word slowly) is <u>baby</u>.*

|  | Pre | Post |
|---|---|---|
| earphones | _____ | _____ |
| treehouse | _____ | _____ |
| picture | _____ | _____ |
| magnet | _____ | _____ |
| calendar | _____ | _____ |

Percent Correct    ⬜/5 %    ⬜/5 %

*Say each word so I can hear each sound,*
*like <u>a-p-l</u> (say the sounds slowly) is <u>apple</u>.*

|  | Pre | Post |
|---|---|---|
| fish | _____ | _____ |
| cup | _____ | _____ |
| phone | _____ | _____ |
| clock | _____ | _____ |
| speech | _____ | _____ |

Percent Correct    ⬜/5 %    ⬜/5 %

#BK-330 Say & Glue® Phonological Awareness • ©2006 Super Duper® Publications • 1-800-277-8737 • www.superduperinc.com

# Phonological Awareness Criterion Test

## Syllable Counting

*Clap one time for each word part you hear (demonstrate the word "paper" – 2 claps).*
*(For this section, add the two columns together to calculate a percentage correct.)*

|  | Pre | Post |  |  | Pre | Post |
|---|---|---|---|---|---|---|
| **shoe** (1) | _____ | _____ |  | **shampoo** (2) | _____ | _____ |
| **jukebox** (2) | _____ | _____ |  | **popular** (3) | _____ | _____ |
| **lap** (1) | _____ | _____ |  | **stationary** (4) | _____ | _____ |
| **horrible** (3) | _____ | _____ |  | **speaker** (2) | _____ | _____ |
| **reverie** (3) | _____ | _____ |  | **graduation** (4) | _____ | _____ |

Percent Correct ⬜ 10 % ⬜ 10 %

## Letter Sounds

*Tell me which word <u>starts</u> with the same sound as the first word I say.*

|  | Pre | Post |
|---|---|---|
| **light** - car, lamb, hot | _____ | _____ |
| **sun** - pot, fan, sit | _____ | _____ |
| **toy** - look, man, top | _____ | _____ |
| **boy** - bat, door, cow | _____ | _____ |
| **catch** - keep, top, it | _____ | _____ |

Percent Correct ⬜ 5 % ⬜ 5 %

*Tell me which word <u>ends</u> with the same sound as the first word I say.*

|  | Pre | Post |
|---|---|---|
| **sip** - tap, low, fun | _____ | _____ |
| **mad** - rock, on, dad | _____ | _____ |
| **buzz** - one, like, toes | _____ | _____ |
| **ham** - go, him, far | _____ | _____ |
| **bag** - pig, farm, cap | _____ | _____ |

Percent Correct ⬜ 5 % ⬜ 5 %

*Tell me the <u>beginning sound</u> of the word I say.*

|  | Pre | Post |
|---|---|---|
| bush | _____ | _____ |
| dog | _____ | _____ |
| goat | _____ | _____ |
| cat | _____ | _____ |
| fox | _____ | _____ |

Percent Correct ⬜ 5 % ⬜ 5 %

*Tell me the <u>ending sound</u> of the word I say.*

|  | Pre | Post |
|---|---|---|
| ball | _____ | _____ |
| hop | _____ | _____ |
| late | _____ | _____ |
| thumb | _____ | _____ |
| house | _____ | _____ |

Percent Correct ⬜ 5 % ⬜ 5 %

# Phonological Awareness Criterion Test

## Deletion of Phonemes

*I am going to ask you to say a word and then say it again without one of its parts.*
(For this section, add the two columns together to calculate a percentage correct.)

|  | Pre | Post |  | Pre | Post |
|---|---|---|---|---|---|
| **doorbell** (door) | _____ | _____ | **happy** (py) | _____ | _____ |
| **snowball** (ball) | _____ | _____ | **reading** (ing) | _____ | _____ |
| **birthday** (birth) | _____ | _____ | **make** (ke) | _____ | _____ |
| **headphones** (phones) | _____ | _____ | **pot** (p) | _____ | _____ |
| **umbrella** (brella) | _____ | _____ | **up** (u) | _____ | _____ |

Percent Correct    10 %    10 %

## Addition of Phonemes

*I am going to ask you to say a word and then say it again adding another part to make a new word.*
(For this section, add the two columns together to calculate a percentage correct.)

|  | Pre | Post |  | Pre | Post |
|---|---|---|---|---|---|
| **apple** (sauce) | _____ | _____ | **pen** (cil) | _____ | _____ |
| **lady** (bug) | _____ | _____ | **ly** (ing) | _____ | _____ |
| **short** (cut) | _____ | _____ | **crack** (er) | _____ | _____ |
| **bed** (time) | _____ | _____ | **pill** (ow) | _____ | _____ |
| **story** (book) | _____ | _____ | **fur** (ry) | _____ | _____ |

Percent Correct    10 %    10 %

## Manipulation of Phonemes

*I am going to ask you to say a word and then say it again. This time, say it with a <u>different</u> sound.*

|  | Pre | Post |  | Pre | Post |
|---|---|---|---|---|---|
| Change "r" in **ram** to "h" | _____ | _____ | Change "u" in **rub** to "i" | _____ | _____ |
| Change "l" in **lid** to "k" | _____ | _____ | Change "s" in **rose** to "p" | _____ | _____ |
| Change "b" in **bat** to "s" | _____ | _____ | Change "i" in **click** to "o" | _____ | _____ |
| Change "t" in **cat** to "p" | _____ | _____ | Change "a" in **pan** to "e" | _____ | _____ |
| Change "l" in **feel** to "t" | _____ | _____ | Change "o" in **rock** to "a" | _____ | _____ |
| Change "t" in **rat** to "m" | _____ | _____ | Change "o" in **wore** to "i" | _____ | _____ |

Percent Correct    12 %    12 %

#BK-330 Say & Glue® Phonological Awareness • ©2006 Super Duper® Publications • 1-800-277-8737 • www.superduperinc.com

# On the Farm

**Directions:** Cut along the dotted line and give the bottom sheet to the student. Have the student cut out the pictures. As you read each nonsense word aloud, the student glues/tapes or places the rhyming pictures on the scene *(horse, pig, cow, pitchfork, hay, tractor)* and then colors the scene.

**Nonsense Words:**   norse      tig      zow      tichfork      tay      nactor

_____        _____        _____
            Name                                    Date                                  Helper

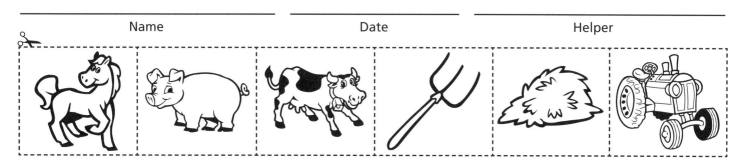

# A Winter Day

**Directions:** Cut along the dotted line and give the bottom sheet to the student. Have the student cut out the pictures. As you read each nonsense word aloud, the student glues/tapes or places the rhyming pictures on the scene *(hat, snowball, smoke, sled, tree, snowman)* and then colors the scene.

**Nonsense Words:**    zat    boball    toke    ked    pree    toman

Name _____    Date _____    Helper _____

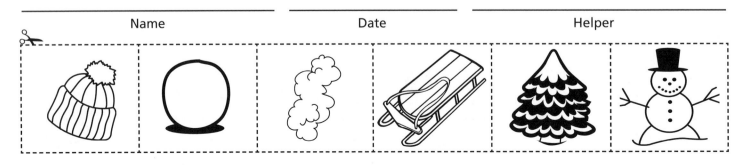

 **Rhyming with Nonsense Words**    #BK-330 Say & Glue® Phonological Awareness    ©2006 Super Duper® Publications • 1-800-277-8737 • www.superduperinc.com

# A Spring Day

**Directions:** Cut along the dotted line and give the bottom sheet to the student. Have the student cut out the pictures. As you read each nonsense word aloud, the student glues/tapes or places the rhyming pictures on the scene *(flowers, grass, worm, sun, bee, bird)* and then colors the scene.

**Nonsense Words:**     nowers     dass     lurm     tun     dee     dird

Name                Date                Helper

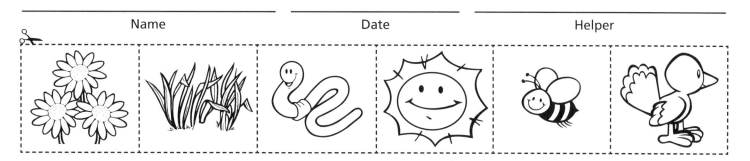

# Garage

**Directions:** Cut along the dotted line and give the bottom sheet to the student. Have the student cut out the pictures. As you read each nonsense word aloud, the student glues/tapes or places the rhyming pictures on the scene *(oil, tire, tool, jack, door, light)* and then colors the scene.

**Nonsense Words:**  moil  pire  zool  dack  noor  yight

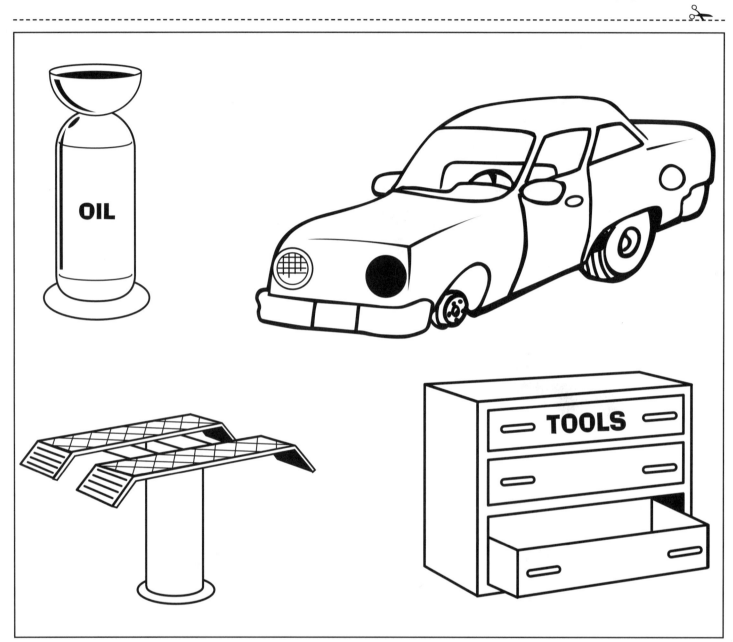

| Name | Date | Helper |
| --- | --- | --- |

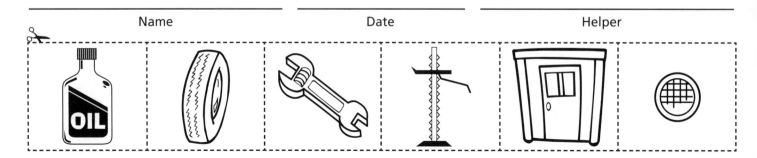

 **Rhyming with Nonsense Words**  #BK-330  Say & Glue® Phonological Awareness  •  ©2006 Super Duper® Publications  •  1-800-277-8737  •  www.superduperinc.com

# Car Wash

**Directions:** Cut along the dotted line and give the bottom sheet to the student. Have the student cut out the pictures. As you read each nonsense word aloud, the student glues/tapes or places the rhyming pictures on the scene *(soap, sponge, puddle, rag, man, wax)* and then colors the scene.

**Nonsense Words:**    tope    nunge    ruddle    dag    han    vax

Name _____    Date _____    Helper _____

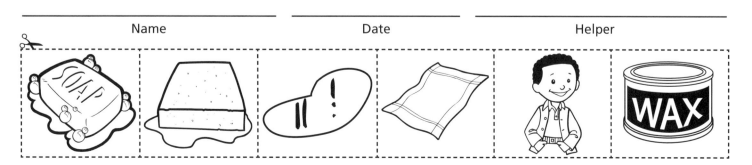

# Party Time

**Directions:** Cut along the dotted line and give the bottom sheet to the student. Have the student cut out the pictures. As you read each nonsense word aloud, the student glues/tapes or places the rhyming pictures on the scene *(hat, cake, gift, candy, horn, drink)* and then colors the scene.

**Nonsense Words:**    jat    zake    nift    tandy    forn    tink

Name          Date          Helper

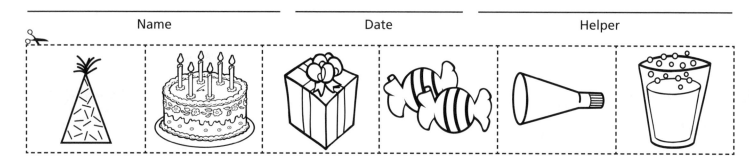

 **Rhyming with Nonsense Words**   #BK-330 Say & Glue® Phonological Awareness • ©2006 Super Duper® Publications • 1-800-277-8737 • www.superduperinc.com

# Dog Show

**Directions:** Cut along the dotted line and give the bottom sheet to the student. Have the student cut out the pictures. As you read each nonsense word aloud, the student glues/tapes or places the rhyming pictures on the scene (*dog, ribbon, leash, girl, brush, bone*) and then colors the scene.

**Nonsense Words:**     nog     tibbon     teash     dirl     dush     sone

Name                    Date                    Helper

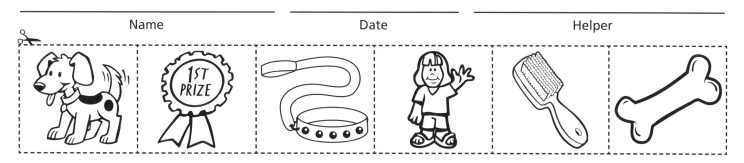

# Jungle Fun

**Directions:** Cut along the dotted line and give the bottom sheet to the student. Have the student cut out the pictures. As you read each nonsense word aloud, the student glues/tapes or places the rhyming pictures on the scene *(toucan, snake, tiger, vine, grass, leopard)* and then colors the scene.

**Nonsense Words:**     roocan     pake     diger     bine     tass     deopard

Name           Date           Helper

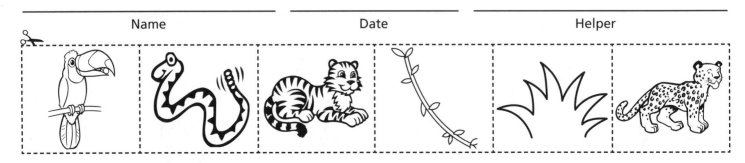

   #BK-330 Say & Glue® Phonological Awareness • ©2006 Super Duper® Publications • 1-800-277-8737 • www.superduperinc.com

# Race Track

**Directions:** Cut along the dotted line and give the bottom sheet to the student. Have the student cut out the pictures. As you read each nonsense word aloud, the student glues/tapes or places the rhyming pictures on the scene (*gas, flag, tire, jack, blimp, car*) and then colors the scene.

**Nonsense Words:** das zag nire dack timp dar

Name            Date            Helper

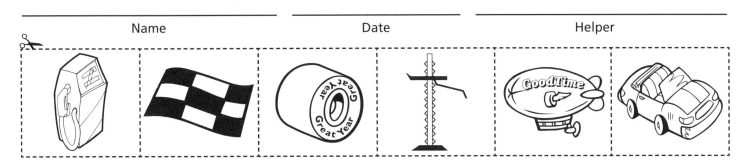

# In the Park

**Directions:** Cut along the dotted line and give the bottom sheet to the student. Have the student cut out the pictures. As you read each nonsense word aloud, the student glues/tapes or places the rhyming pictures on the scene *(tree, bike, swing, sun, sand, bench)* and then colors the scene.

**Nonsense Words:**   ree   nike   ting   cun   nand   nench

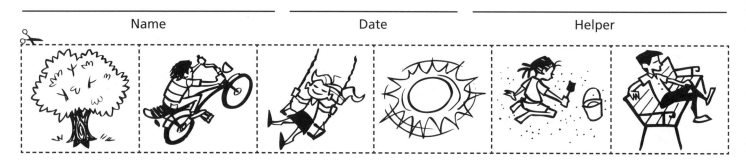

_____   _____   _____
Name                                        Date                                          Helper

 #BK-330 Say & Glue® Phonological Awareness • ©2006 Super Duper® Publications • 1-800-277-8737 • www.superduperinc.com

# Rhyming Sentences

   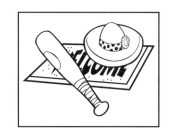

# Silly Sentences

**Directions:** Cut along the dotted line and give the bottom sheet to the student. Have the student cut out the pictures. Helper reads the rhyming word. The student finds two pictures that rhyme with the word and glues/tapes or places them in each sentence *(bib, crib, neck, check, calf, half, day, play)*.

**rib**

The baby with the _____ hurt his **rib** falling out of the _____ .

**deck**

The man with the big _____ had a _____ on the **deck**.

**laugh**

The boy had to **laugh** when his _____ ate _____ of his pie.

**stay**

We could **stay** all _____ and _____ .

_____  _____  _____
Name  Date  Helper

# Rhyming Riddles

**Directions:** Cut along the dotted line and give the bottom sheet to the student. Have the student cut out the pictures. Helper reads the rhyming word. The student finds two pictures that rhyme with the word and glues/tapes or places them in each sentence *(men, hen, stick, brick, bread, bed, flag, bag)*.

✂ - - - - - - - - - - - - - - - - - - - - - - - - - - - - - - - - - - - - - - - - - - - - - - - - - - - - - - - - - - - - - - - - - -

**pen**

The two _____ were in the **pen** with the _____ .

**kick**

She didn't mean to **kick** the _____ or the _____.

**fed**

He **fed** the dog _____ on the _____ .

**wag**

The dog with the _____ and the _____ likes to **wag** his tail.

_____   _____   _____
Name                          Date                          Helper

# Radical Rhymes

**Directions:** Cut along the dotted line and give the bottom sheet to the student. Have the student cut out the pictures. Helper reads the rhyming word. The student finds two pictures that rhyme with the word and glues/tapes or places them in each sentence *(sled, bed, sweat, jet, bell, shell, gold, cold)*.

**head**

I hit my **head** when I put the _____ under my _____.

**wet**

I got **wet** with _____ when I watched the _____.

**smell**

I tried to **smell** the _____ and the _____.

**sold**

He **sold** the _____ in the _____.

_____     _____     _____
Name                                          Date                                           Helper

# Sassy Sentences

**Directions:** Cut along the dotted line and give the bottom sheet to the student. Have the student cut out the pictures. Helper reads the rhyming word. The student finds two pictures that rhyme with the word and glues/tapes or places them in each sentence *(bee, knee, braid, shade, peach, beach, fry, cry).*

**see**

I didn't **see** the _____ on my _____.

**paid**

She **paid** to have a _____ in the _____.

**reach**

I had to **reach** for my _____ on the _____.

**guy**

The **guy** with the _____ started to _____.

Name                      Date                      Helper

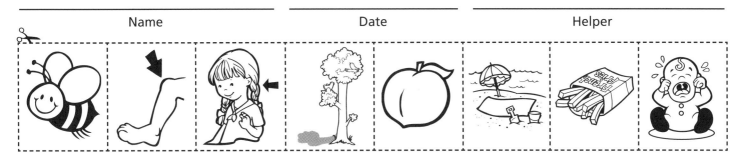

# Rhyme Time

**Directions:** Cut along the dotted line and give the bottom sheet to the student. Have the student cut out the pictures. Helper reads the rhyming word. The student finds two pictures that rhyme with the word and glues/tapes or places them in each sentence *(pot, hot, light, night, Mike, bike, bear, pear)*.

---

**not**

The large _____ was **not** very _____.

**bright**

The bedroom _____ was **bright** in the _____.

**like**

A boy named _____ had a _____ that he did not **like**.

**share**

The fuzzy _____ with the _____ likes to **share**.

_____   _____   _____
Name                                          Date                                          Helper

**Rhyming Sentences** #BK-330 Say & Glue® Phonological Awareness • ©2006 Super Duper® Publications • 1-800-277-8737 • www.superduperinc.com

# Silly Sentences II

**Directions:** Cut along the dotted line and give the bottom sheet to the student. Have the student cut out the pictures. Helper reads the rhyming word. The student finds two pictures that rhyme with the word and glues/tapes or places them in each sentence (*wave, cave, book, hook, boy, toy, hop, mop*).

- - - - - - - - - - - - - - - - - - - - - - - - - - - - - - - - - - - - - - - - - - - - - - - - ✂- - -

**Dave**

<u>Dave</u> gave a _____ and went in the _____.

**took**

He **took** the _____ that was by the _____.

**joy**

The young _____ with the _____ was full of **joy**.

**top**

He had to _____ on **top** of the _____.

_____     _____     _____
Name                                          Date                        Helper

# Rhyming Riddles II

**Directions:** Cut along the dotted line and give the bottom sheet to the student. Have the student cut out the pictures. Helper reads the rhyming word. The student finds two pictures that rhyme with the word and glues/tapes or places them in each sentence *(can, man, four, floor, net, wet, coat, float)*.

**ran**

He **ran** with the _____ all the way to the _____.

**more**

He wanted **more** than _____ blocks on the _____.

**get**

He tried not to **get** the _____ very _____.

**goat**

The **goat** had on a _____ and sat in a _____.

_____     _____     _____
Name                              Date                               Helper

#BK-330 Say & Glue® Phonological Awareness • ©2006 Super Duper® Publications • 1-800-277-8737 • www.superduperinc.com

# Radical Rhymes II

**Directions:** Cut along the dotted line and give the bottom sheet to the student. Have the student cut out the pictures. Helper reads the rhyming word. The student finds two pictures that rhyme with the word and glues/tapes or places them in each sentence *(flea, tree, mat, hat, pig, wig, duck, truck)*.

✂ - - - - - - - - - - - - - - - - - - - - - - - - - - - - - - - - - - - - - - - - - - - - - - - -

**bee**

A **bee** and a _____ sat on a_____ .

**cat**

The **cat** on the _____ was wearing a _____ .

**big**

The **big** _____ wore a _____ .

**stuck**

The _____ was **stuck** near the _____ .

_____     _____     _____
           Name                              Date                      Helper

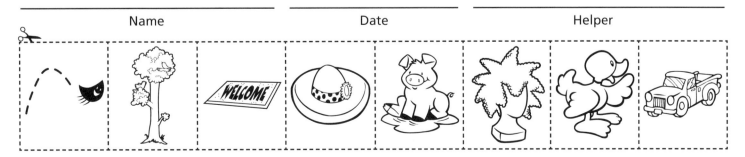

# Sassy Sentences II

**Directions:** Cut along the dotted line and give the bottom sheet to the student. Have the student cut out the pictures. Helper reads the rhyming word. The student finds two pictures that rhyme with the word and glues/tapes or places them in each sentence *(hat, bat, cap, map, Dad, sad, fed, bread)*.

- - - - - - - - - - - - - - - - - - - - - - - - - - - - - - - - - - - - - - - - - - - - - - - - - ✂

**cat**

The **cat** had a _____ and a _____.

**lap**

The _____ and _____ were on my **lap**.

**bad**

When we were **bad,** it made _____ _____.

**Ned**

**Ned** _____ the birds some _____.

_____     _____     _____
Name                              Date                        Helper

#BK-330 Say & Glue® Phonological Awareness • ©2006 Super Duper® Publications • 1-800-277-8737 • www.superduperinc.com

# Rhyme Time II

**Directions:** Cut along the dotted line and give the bottom sheet to the student. Have the student cut out the pictures. Helper reads the rhyming word. The student finds two pictures that rhyme with the word and glues/tapes or places them in each sentence *(fish, dish, hat, mat, soap, rope, hurt, shirt)*.

**wish**

The big _____ in the _____ made a **wish**.

**bat**

My **bat** and _____ are on the _____ .

**hope**

I **hope** the _____ didn't get on the _____ .

**Bert**

**Bert** didn't get _____ when he tore his _____ .

_____    _____    _____
Name                          Date                         Helper

# Silly Sentences III

**Directions:** Cut along the dotted line and give the bottom sheet to the student. Have the student cut out the pictures. Helper reads the rhyming word. The student finds two pictures that rhyme with the word and glues/tapes or places them in each sentence *(dog, hog, skate, late, snow, toe, sack, tack)*.

- - - - - - - - - - - - - - - - - - - - - - - - - - - - - - - - - - - - - - - - - - - - - - - - - - - - - - - - - - ✂

**log**

The _____ ate like a _____ while he sat on the **log**.

**wait**

We have to **wait** to go _____ ; it may be too _____.

**blow**

The _____ began to **blow** and covered each _____.

**back**

I hurt my **back** when I tripped on the _____ and fell on the _____.

Name _____ Date _____ Helper _____

#BK-330 Say & Glue® Phonological Awareness • ©2006 Super Duper® Publications • 1-800-277-8737 • www.superduperinc.com

# Fill in the Rhyming Word

# City Street

**Directions:** Cut along the dotted line and give the bottom sheet to the student. Have the student cut out the pictures. Helper reads a sentence. The student finds a picture that makes the sentence rhyme, says it aloud, and glues/tapes or places it on the scene *(store, bike, cat, sign, light, sack)*.

1. When I go in, I always want **more**. It's fun to look around in the toy _____.

2. This one belongs to a boy named **Mike**. He loves to ride his two-wheeled _____.

3. He says meow. He's not very **fat**. I love to pet the little _____.

4. This makes the cars stop in a **line**. It's on a pole. It's a red stop _____.

5. Its colors shine very **bright**. Stop and go, watch the traffic _____.

6. You can't wear this on your **back**. Put your food in a grocery _____.

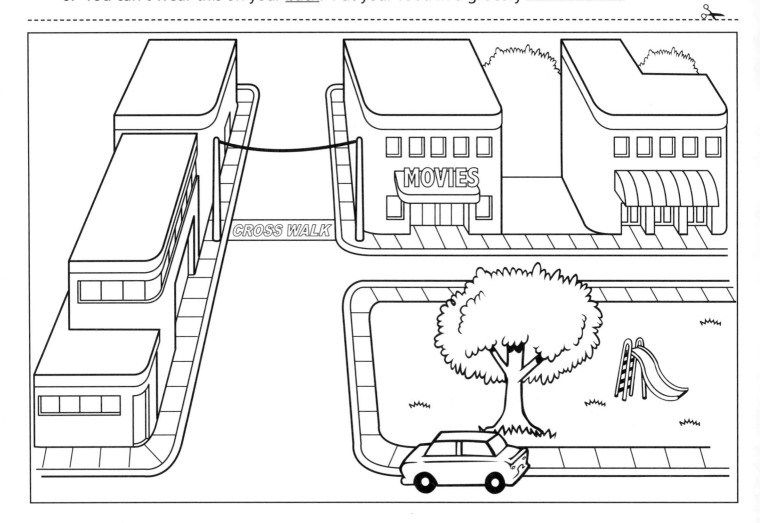

Name _____  Date _____  Helper _____

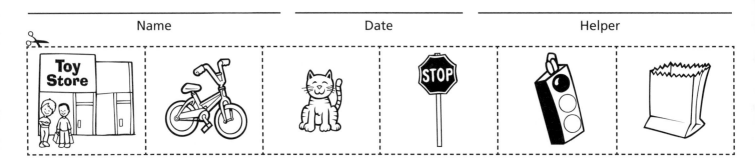

 #BK-330 Say & Glue® Phonological Awareness • ©2006 Super Duper® Publications • 1-800-277-8737 • www.superduperinc.com

# Circus Fun

**Directions:** Cut along the dotted line and give the bottom sheet to the student.  Have the student cut out the pictures. Helper reads a sentence.  The student finds a picture that makes the sentence rhyme, says it aloud, and glues/tapes or places it on the scene *(clown, bear, bike, ball, bone, candy)*.

1. They came from all over **town** just to see the silly _____.

2. It is quite **rare** to see such a funny _____.

3. This is what we all **like**, when the man on the highwire rides his _____.

4. They listen to their trainer **call**, as the seals pass around the colorful _____.

5. They get excited when this is **shown**.  All dogs love to work for a delicious _____.

6. The man was very **handy** at selling cotton _____.

_____      _____      _____
Name                                              Date                                              Helper

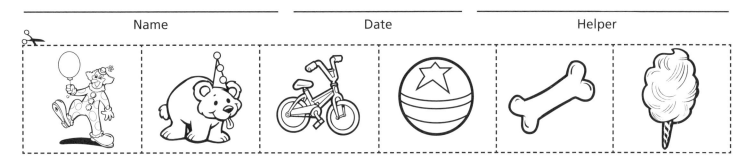

# In the Zoo

**Directions:** Cut along the dotted line and give the bottom sheet to the student. Have the student cut out the pictures. Helper reads a sentence. The student finds a picture that makes the sentence rhyme, says it aloud, and glues/tapes or places it on the scene (*nest, snake, fish, bird, boy, seal*).

1. It's time to sit and take a <u>rest</u>. Let's watch the birds in their _____.
2. A hissing sound it likes to <u>make</u>. I love to go and see the _____.
3. His tail goes back and forth with a <u>swish</u>. Look in the water and see a _____.
4. The prettiest song that I ever <u>heard</u> came from a pretty, little _____.
5. He wants to buy a new <u>toy</u>. It's not a girl, it's a _____.
6. His loud bark is not a <u>squeal</u>. You can always hear the funny _____.

Name            Date            Helper

**Fill in the Rhyming Word**    #BK-330 Say & Glue® Phonological Awareness  •  ©2006 Super Duper® Publications  •  1-800-277-8737  •  www.superduperinc.com

# Grocery Store

**Directions:** Cut along the dotted line and give the bottom sheet to the student. Have the student cut out the pictures. Helper reads a sentence. The student finds a picture that makes the sentence rhyme, says it aloud, and glues/tapes or places it on the scene *(cherry, pear, chips, bread, cup, pie)*.

1. It tastes kind of like a **berry**. I like to eat a big, red _____.

2. This is a good treat to **share**... a big, fat, juicy _____.

3. They taste great with different **dips**. I love to eat potato _____.

4. I don't want it on my **head**. I want the butter on my _____.

5. I love to fill it **up**. It's my big, red plastic _____.

6. Oh me, oh **my**, I love to eat _____.

Name _____     Date _____     Helper _____

# The Big City

**Directions:** Cut along the dotted line and give the bottom sheet to the student. Have the student cut out the pictures. Helper reads a sentence. The student finds a picture that makes the sentence rhyme, says it aloud, and glues/tapes or places it on the scene *(bus, plane, van, wreck, cab, train)*.

1. Sometimes the kids on here will **<u>fuss</u>**, as they ride to school on the _____.
2. It can't fly if there's too much **<u>rain</u>**, but it's fun to look up and see a _____.
3. He is such a busy **<u>man</u>**. The plumber drives to work in his _____.
4. He hurt his **<u>neck</u>** after the car _____.
5. You must pay a **<u>tab</u>** for riding in the _____.
6. Instead of fighting traffic in the **<u>lane</u>**, we will take the _____.

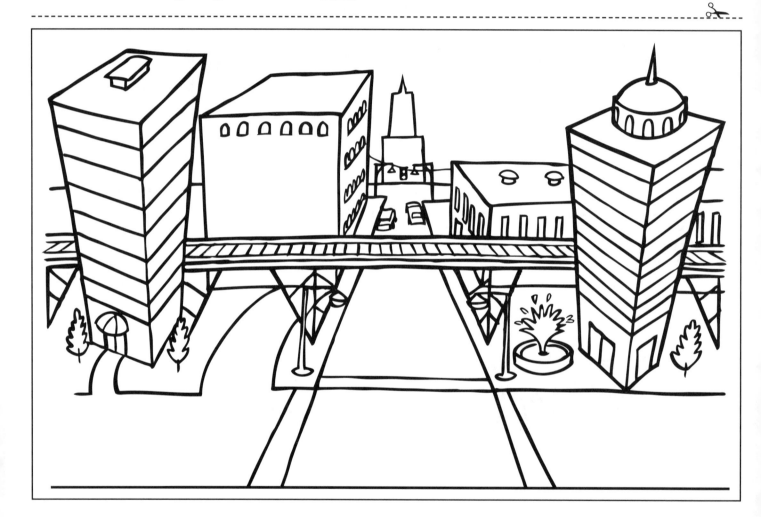

| Name | Date | Helper |
|------|------|--------|

Fill in the Rhyming Word    #BK-330 Say & Glue® Phonological Awareness • ©2006 Super Duper® Publications • 1-800-277-8737 • www.superduperinc.com

# On the Beach

**Directions:** Cut along the dotted line and give the bottom sheet to the student. Have the student cut out the pictures. Helper reads a sentence. The student finds a picture that makes the sentence rhyme, says it aloud, and glues/tapes or places it on the scene *(sun, boat, shell, swim, hand, ball)*.

1. We can have lots of <u>fun</u> outdoors in the _____.

2. While in the water on a <u>float</u>, we might see a big, fast _____.

3. Rashan almost <u>fell</u> when he stepped on the big _____.

4. I will have fun with Austin and <u>Jim</u>, as we splash and play while we _____.

5. As I sit on the beach in the <u>sand</u>, I will build a castle with my _____.

6. I'll be careful not to <u>fall</u> when I chase the big, round _____.

_____  _____  _____
         Name                         Date                      Helper

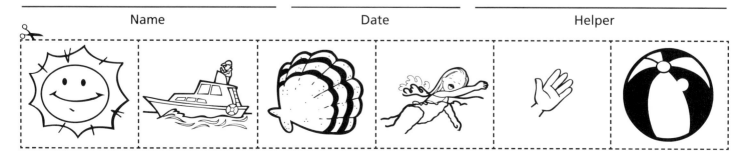

# School Days

**Directions:** Cut along the dotted line and give the bottom sheet to the student. Have the student cut out the pictures. Helper reads a sentence. The student finds a picture that makes the sentence rhyme, says it aloud, and glues/tapes or places it on the scene *(chair, board, backpack, flag, book, write)*.

1. Mad because they didn't play **fair**, the boy sulked in his _____.
2. I can draw a long **sword**, if I draw it on the _____.
3. It holds objects like a **sack**. I carry books in my _____.
4. After school, we like to play **tag** around the big, American _____.
5. She sat down to **look** at the picture _____.
6. Hold your pencil **tight** when you get ready to _____.

Name        Date        Helper

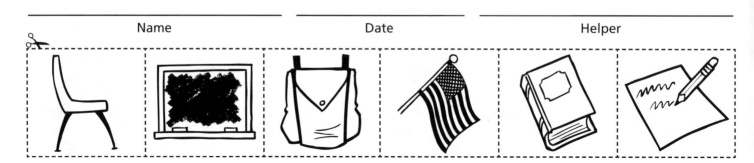

# At the Market

**Directions:** Cut along the dotted line and give the bottom sheet to the student. Have the student cut out the pictures. Helper reads a sentence. The student finds a picture that makes the sentence rhyme, says it aloud, and glues/tapes or places it on the scene *(milk, bread, cheese, salt, flour, ham)*.

1. It's as smooth as **silk**. I love to drink _____.

2. Nobody smiles as big as **Ted** when he eats _____.

3. It makes me **wheeze** when I eat _____.

4. It's not my **fault** I spilled the _____.

5. To make a cake as big as a **tower**, you must first add _____.

6. Instead of cooking **lamb**, Mom made a big _____.

_____     _____     _____
Name                      Date                    Helper

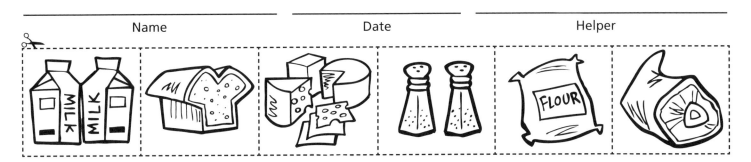

# In the Yard

**Directions:** Cut along the dotted line and give the bottom sheet to the student. Have the student cut out the pictures. Helper reads a sentence. The student finds a picture that makes the sentence rhyme, says it aloud, and glues/tapes or places it on the scene *(roses, ball, bat, dog, mailbox, grass)*.

1. They used their **noses** to smell the beautiful _____.
2. Latasha didn't want to go to the **mall**. She only wanted a _____.
3. You wear a special **hat** when you hit the ball with a _____.
4. Jeff will have to step over the **log** in order to get to the barking _____.
5. There are lots of pretty **rocks** around the bottom of the _____.
6. Please do not leave your **glass** sitting in the _____.

Name _____     Date _____     Helper _____

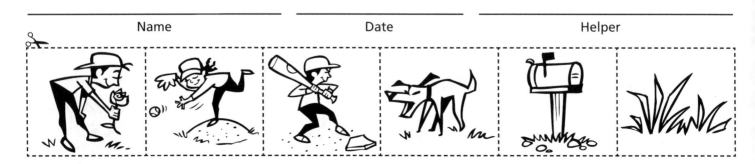

 #BK-330 Say & Glue® Phonological Awareness • ©2006 Super Duper® Publications • 1-800-277-8737 • www.superduperinc.com

# On the Playground

**Directions:** Cut along the dotted line and give the bottom sheet to the student. Have the student cut out the pictures. Helper reads a sentence. The student finds a picture that makes the sentence rhyme, says it aloud, and glues/tapes or places it on the scene *(swing, pail, bench, ball, kite, sand)*.

1. The children laugh and **sing** as they ride on the great big _____.

2. Shane had to **bail** sand out of the _____.

3. The lady was speaking **French,** as she sat upon the wooden _____.

4. If you are **tall,** you can really shoot the _____.

5. You should hold on very **tight** when you go to fly your _____.

6. Ava reached out her **hand** to play in the _____.

_____     _____     _____
Name                                    Date                                  Helper

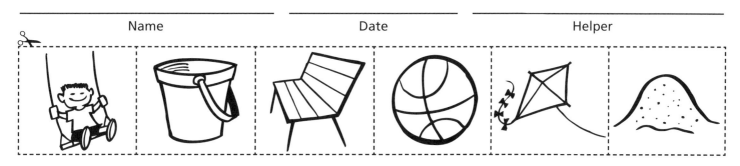

# The Mall

**Directions:** Cut along the dotted line and give the bottom sheet to the student. Have the student cut out the pictures. Helper reads a sentence. The student finds a picture that makes the sentence rhyme, says it aloud, and glues/tapes or places it on the scene *(ball, candy, seat, buy, store, more)*.

1. When I went to Columbia **Mall**, my Daddy bought me a big, red _____.
2. Yum-yum! It's really **dandy** to buy lots of yummy _____.
3. After I get something to **eat**, I look around to find a _____.
4. There is a balloon way up **high** that I would like money to _____.
5. It's always fun, never a **bore**, when I go to the toy _____.
6. As I see new things in the toy **store**, I want _____!

Name _____    Date _____    Helper _____

**Fill in the Rhyming Word** #BK-330 Say & Glue® Phonological Awareness • ©2006 Super Duper® Publications • 1-800-277-8737 • www.superduperinc.com

# Which Rhyming Word Belongs?

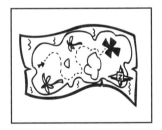   

# Rhyme Time

**Directions:** Cut along the dotted line and give the bottom sheet to the student. Have the student cut out the pictures. Helper reads the rhyming words. The student finds the picture that rhymes with the words, says them aloud, and glues/tapes or places them in the boxes *(mop, book, boat, ring, vest)*.

1. **STOP** stop     top

2. hook     cook

3. coat     goat

4. swing     king

5. nest     **N W←E S** west

| Name | Date | Helper |
|---|---|---|

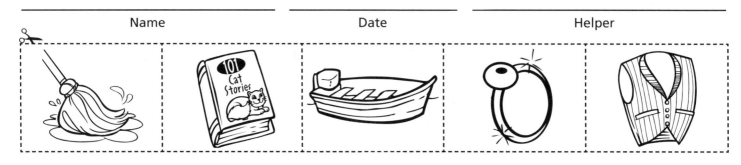

 Which Rhyming Word Belongs?   #BK-330 Say & Glue® Phonological Awareness   ©2006 Super Duper® Publications • 1-800-277-8737 • www.superduperinc.com

# Rhyming Fun

**Directions:** Cut along the dotted line and give the bottom sheet to the student.  Have the student cut out the pictures.  Helper reads the rhyming words.  The student finds the picture that rhymes with the words, says them aloud, and glues/tapes or places them in the boxes *(dice, wheel, sheep, shell, ten)*.

1. | ice | mice | |

2. | heel | peel | |

3. | jeep | sleep | |

4. | bell | well | |

5. | men | pen | |

_____ Name   _____ Date   _____ Helper

# Sounds Like...

**Directions:** Cut along the dotted line and give the bottom sheet to the student. Have the student cut out the pictures. Helper reads the rhyming words. The student finds the picture that rhymes with the words, says them aloud, and glues/tapes or places them in the boxes (*bow, store, bank, map, cash*).

1. | mow | snow | |

2. | tore | more | |

3. | crank | tank | |

4. | cap | lap | |

5. | rash | mash | |

Name          Date          Helper

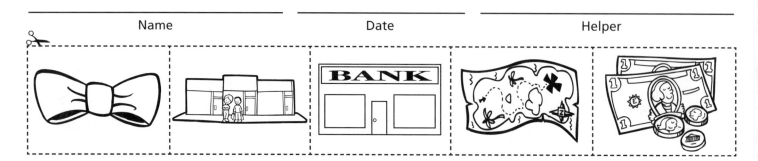

Which Rhyming Word Belongs?    #BK-330 Say & Glue® Phonological Awareness • ©2006 Super Duper® Publications • 1-800-277-8737 • www.superduperinc.com

# Cool Rhymes

**Directions:** Cut along the dotted line and give the bottom sheet to the student. Have the student cut out the pictures. Helper reads the rhyming words. The student finds the picture that rhymes with the words, says them aloud, and glues/tapes or places them in the boxes (*gate, saw, hay, sack, mad*).

1. **eight**     **plate**

2. **straw**     **paw**

3. **play**     **day**

4. **tack**     **pack**

5. **sad**     **dad**

Name      Date      Helper

# Line by Line Rhyme

**Directions:** Cut along the dotted line and give the bottom sheet to the student. Have the student cut out the pictures. Helper reads the rhyming words. The student finds the picture that rhymes with the words, says them aloud, and glues/tapes or places them in the boxes (*rain, ball, jam, fan, cake*).

1. train  | pain

2. call  | tall

3. ham  | slam

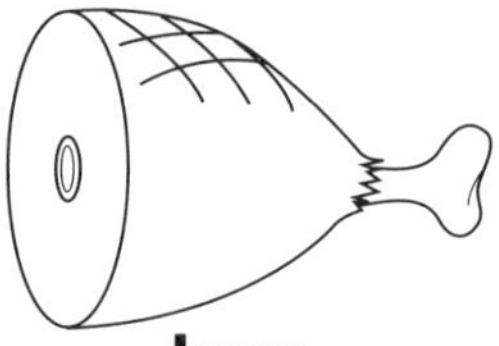

4. can  | tan

5. lake  | rake

Name

Date

Helper

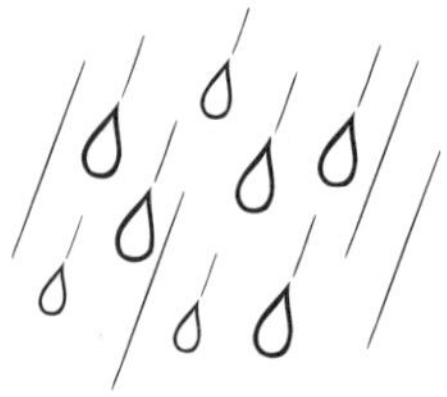

**Which Rhyming Word Belongs?** #BK-330 Say & Glue® Phonological Awareness • ©2006 Super Duper® Publications • 1-800-277-8737 • www.superduperinc.com

# Rhyme Time II

**Directions:** Cut along the dotted line and give the bottom sheet to the student. Have the student cut out the pictures. Helper reads the rhyming words. The student finds the picture that rhymes with the words, says them aloud, and glues/tapes or places them in the boxes *(zipper, platter, teachers, wrinkle, flower)*.

1. slipper | dipper | ⬚

2. batter | shatter | ⬚

3. bleachers | creatures | ⬚

4. sprinkle | twinkle | ⬚

5. tower | power | ⬚

_____    _____    _____
Name         Date         Helper

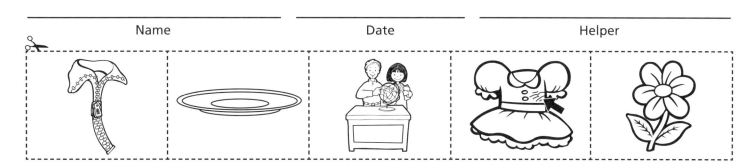

# Rhyming Fun II

**Directions:** Cut along the dotted line and give the bottom sheet to the student. Have the student cut out the pictures. Helper reads the rhyming words. The student finds the picture that rhymes with the words, says them aloud, and glues/tapes or places them in the boxes *(sister, money, rocket, rattle, tickle)*.

1. twister | blister | 

2. bunny | honey | 

3. pocket | socket | 

4. paddle | saddle | 

5. nickel | pickle | 

Name      Date      Helper

#BK-330 Say & Glue® Phonological Awareness • ©2006 Super Duper® Publications • 1-800-277-8737 • www.superduperinc.com

# Sounds Like... II

**Directions:** Cut along the dotted line and give the bottom sheet to the student. Have the student cut out the pictures. Helper reads the rhyming words. The student finds the picture that rhymes with the words, says them aloud, and glues/tapes or places them in the boxes *(table, candle, dryer, rocker, splinter)*.

1. cable      label

2. handle      sandal

3. higher      flyer

4. locker      soccer

5. winter      printer

Name          Date          Helper

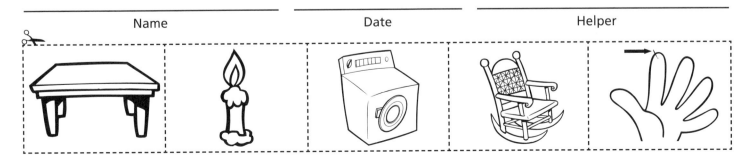

# Cool Rhymes II

**Directions:** Cut along the dotted line and give the bottom sheet to the student. Have the student cut out the pictures. Helper reads the rhyming words. The student finds the picture that rhymes with the words, says them aloud, and glues/tapes or places them in the boxes (*wrapping, apple, laces, skater, waving*).

1. clapping    snapping

2. chapel    scalpel

3. braces    faces

4. waiter    straighter

5. saving    shaving

Name          Date          Helper

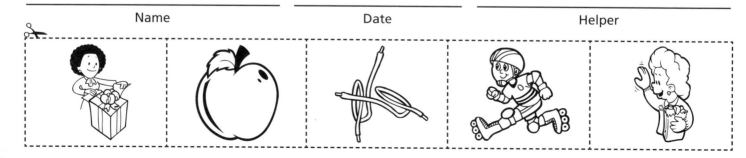

Which Rhyming Word Belongs?    #BK-330  Say & Glue® Phonological Awareness  • ©2006 Super Duper® Publications • 1-800-277-8737 • www.superduperinc.com

# Line by Line Rhyme II

**Directions:** Cut along the dotted line and give the bottom sheet to the student. Have the student cut out the pictures. Helper reads the rhyming words. The student finds the picture that rhymes with the words, says them aloud, and glues/tapes or places them in the boxes *(reading, peeking, blender, heater, sliding)*.

1. feeding     bleeding

2. speaking     leaking

3. slender     fender

4. beater     liter

5. hiding     riding

Name       Date       Helper

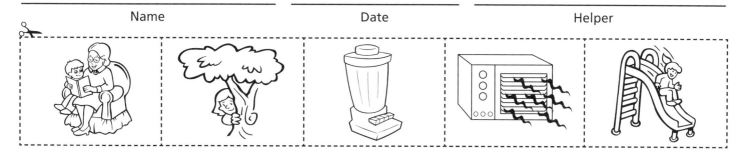

# Rhyme Time III

**Directions:** Cut along the dotted line and give the bottom sheet to the student. Have the student cut out the pictures. Helper reads the rhyming words. The student finds the picture that rhymes with the words, says them aloud, and glues/tapes or places them in the boxes (*middle, crying, kicking, nickel, honey*).

1. fiddle  | griddle | [ ]

2. flying 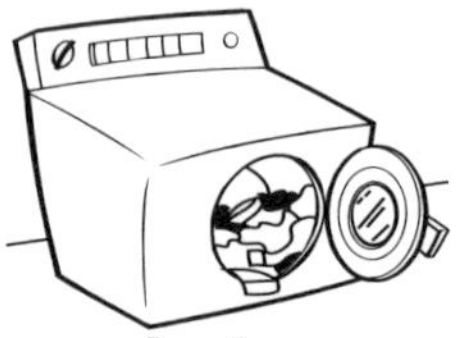 | drying | [ ]

3. picking  | licking | [ ]

4. pickle  | tickle | [ ]

5. money  | sunny | [ ]

Name _____  Date _____  Helper _____

# Blending Syllables/Phonemes

# In the Park

**Directions:** Cut along the dotted line and give the bottom sheet to the student. Have the student cut out the pictures. Helper says each word in its separate parts. The student says the word parts <u>together</u> to make a new word. Then, the student glues/tapes or places the new word on the scene.

**Teacher/Helper says:**   base-ball    see-saw    bas-ket    chil-dren    run-ning    fris-bee

Name _____    Date _____    Helper _____

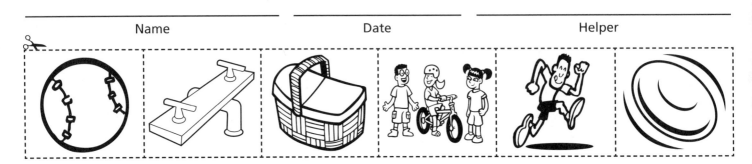

 **Blending Syllables/Phonemes**    #BK-330 Say & Glue® Phonological Awareness • ©2006 Super Duper® Publications • 1-800-277-8737 • www.superduperinc.com

# Party Time

**Directions:** Cut along the dotted line and give the bottom sheet to the student.  Have the student cut out the pictures.  Helper says each word in its separate parts. The student says the word parts <u>together</u> to make a new word.  Then, the student glues/tapes or places the new word on the scene.

<u>**Teacher/Helper says:**</u>  **cup-cake     pres-ent     prin-cess     stream-er     bal-loon     cook-ie**

Name _____    Date _____    Helper _____

# Fun at School

**Directions:** Cut along the dotted line and give the bottom sheet to the student. Have the student cut out the pictures. Helper says each word in its separate parts. The student says the word parts <u>together</u> to make a new word. Then, the student glues/tapes or places the new word on the scene.

**Teacher/Helper says:**   **pen-cil**   **pa-per**   **book-bag**   **note-book**   **clip-board**   **cray-ons**

Name         Date         Helper

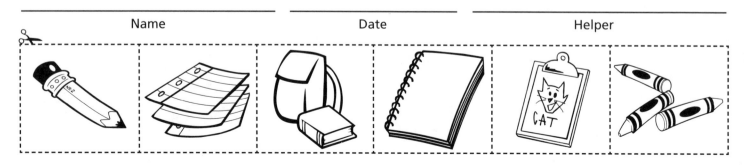

#BK-330 Say & Glue® Phonological Awareness • ©2006 Super Duper® Publications • 1-800-277-8737 • www.superduperinc.com

# Cozy Kitchen

**Directions:** Cut along the dotted line and give the bottom sheet to the student. Have the student cut out the pictures. Helper says each word in its separate parts. The student says the word parts <u>together</u> to make a new word. Then, the student glues/tapes or places the new word on the scene.

<u>**Teacher/Helper says:**</u> **tel-e-phone    mi-cro-wave    sil-ver-ware dish-wash-er    de-ter-gent    cab-i-net**

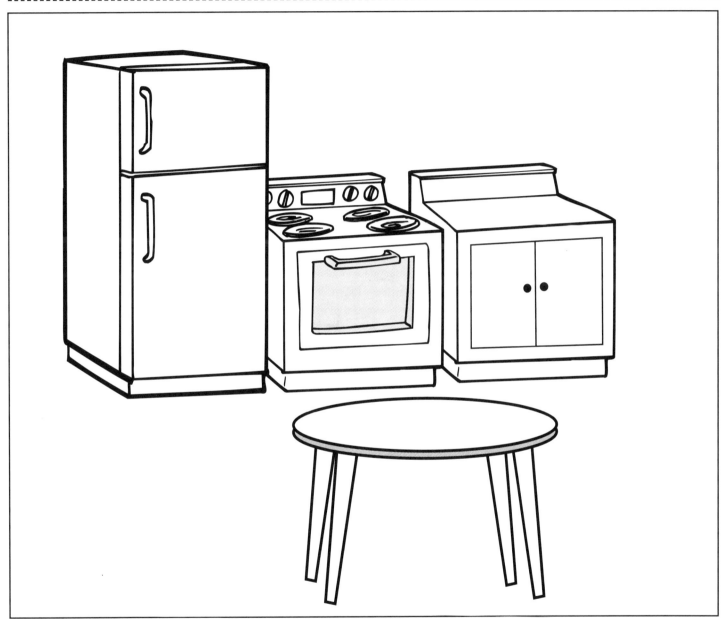

Name          Date          Helper

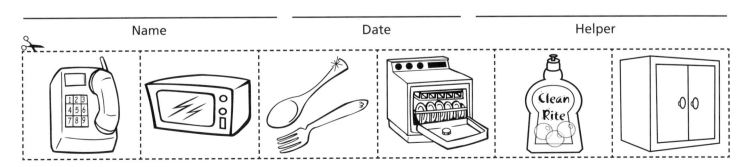

# Fruits and Vegetables

**Directions:** Cut along the dotted line and give the bottom sheet to the student.  Have the student cut out the pictures.  Helper says each word in its separate parts.  The student says the word parts <u>together</u> to make a new word. Then, the student glues/tapes or places the new word on the scene.

<u>**Teacher/Helper says:**</u>  **ba-na-na     pine-ap-ple     straw-ber-ry
can-ta-loupe     po-ta-to     cu-cum-ber**

Name          Date          Helper

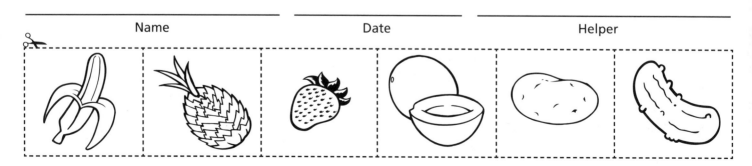

 **Blending Syllables/Phonemes**     #BK-330  Say & Glue® Phonological Awareness  • ©2006 Super Duper® Publications  • 1-800-277-8737 •  www.superduperinc.com

# At the Zoo

**Directions:** Cut along the dotted line and give the bottom sheet to the student. Have the student cut out the pictures. Helper says each word in its separate parts. The student says the word parts <u>together</u> to make a new word. Then, the student glues/tapes or places the new word on the scene.

<u>**Teacher/Helper says:**</u> **go-ril-la    el-e-phant    an-te-lope
chim-pan-zee    pel-i-can    fla-min-go**

Name _____    Date _____    Helper _____

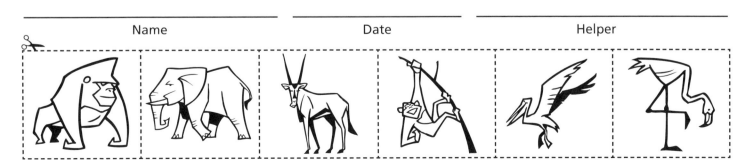

# Playroom Fun

**Directions:** Cut along the dotted line and give the bottom sheet to the student. Have the student cut out the pictures. Helper says each word in its separate parts. The student says the word parts <u>together</u> to make a new word. Then, the student glues/tapes or places the new word on the scene.

**<u>Teacher/Helper says:</u>**    **d-o-ll**   **b-oo-k**   **g-a-me**   **b-a-ll**   **b-l-o-ck-s**   **c-ar**

Name           Date           Helper

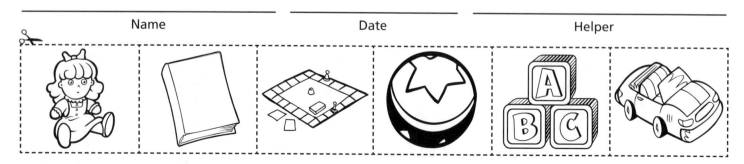

**Blending Syllables/Phonemes**    #BK-330 Say & Glue® Phonological Awareness • ©2006 Super Duper® Publications • 1-800-277-8737 • www.superduperinc.com

# Barnyard Time

**Directions:** Cut along the dotted line and give the bottom sheet to the student. Have the student cut out the pictures. Helper says each word in its separate parts. The student says the word parts <u>together</u> to make a new word. Then, the student glues/tapes or places the new word on the scene.

**<u>Teacher/Helper says:</u>**   c-ow    sh-ee-p    p-i-g    h-or-se    g-oa-t    h-e-n

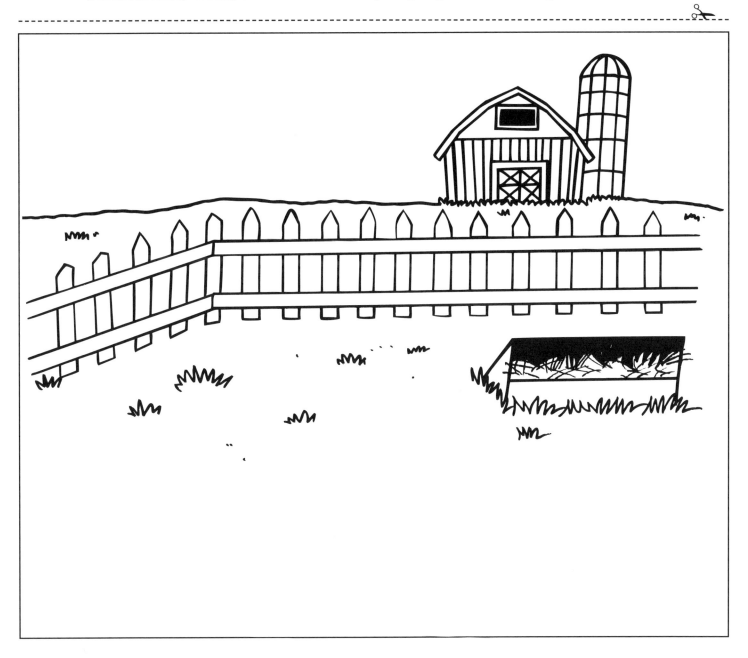

| Name | Date | Helper |
|------|------|--------|

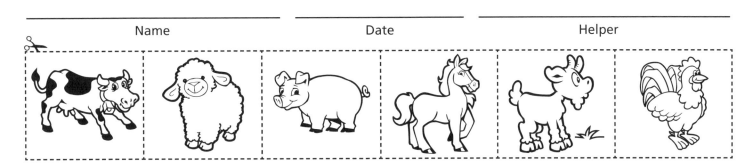

# Music Lesson

**Directions:** Cut along the dotted line and give the bottom sheet to the student. Have the student cut out the pictures. Helper says each word in its separate parts. The student says the word parts <u>together</u> to make a new word. Then, the student glues/tapes or places the new word on the scene.

<u>**Teacher/Helper says:**</u>  **d-r-u-m    h-or-n    k-ey-s    f-l-u-te    n-o-te-s    h-ar-p**

| Name | Date | Helper |
|---|---|---|

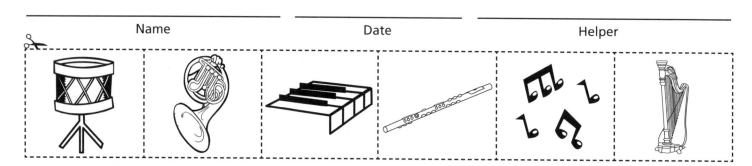

 **Blending Syllables/Phonemes**  #BK-330 Say & Glue® Phonological Awareness • ©2006 Super Duper® Publications • 1-800-277-8737 • www.superduperinc.com

# On the Pond

**Directions:** Cut along the dotted line and give the bottom sheet to the student. Have the student cut out the pictures. Helper says each word in its separate parts. The student says the word parts <u>together</u> to make a new word. Then, the student glues/tapes or places the new word on the scene.

**Teacher/Helper says:**   d-u-ck   b-ir-d   l-o-g   f-r-o-g   s-n-a-ke   sh-r-u-b

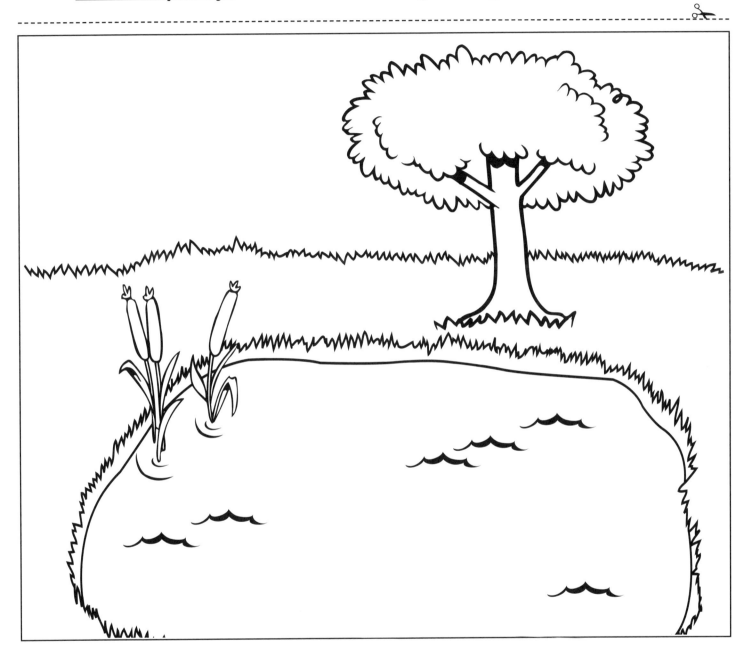

Name            Date            Helper

# Rainy Day

**Directions:** Cut along the dotted line and give the bottom sheet to the student. Have the student cut out the pictures. Helper says each word in its separate parts. The student says the word parts <u>together</u> to make a new word. Then, the student glues/tapes or places the new word on the scene.

<u>**Teacher/Helper says:**</u>   b-oo-t-s   c-oa-t   m-u-d   r-ai-n   f-i-sh   h-a-t

| Name | Date | Helper |
|---|---|---|

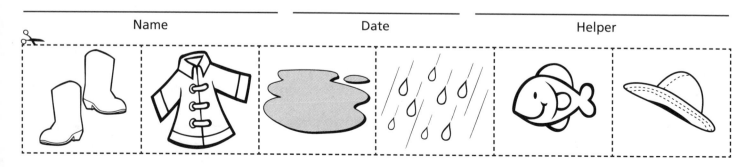

 **Blending Syllables/Phonemes**   #BK-330  Say & Glue® Phonological Awareness  •  ©2006 Super Duper® Publications  •  1-800-277-8737  •  www.superduperinc.com

# Segmentation

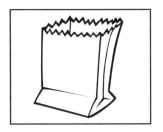   

  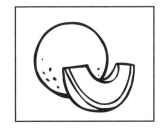 

# Word Wonders

**Directions:** Cut along the dotted line and give the bottom sheet to the student. Have the student cut out the pictures. Helper says a compound word. The student says the two words that make up the word. The student finds the pictures for the compound word and glues/tapes or places them on the page.

**Teacher/Helper says:** **rainbow**    **football**    **armchair**    **bagpipe**    **barnyard**    **bulldog**

_____      _____      _____
Name                 Date                Helper

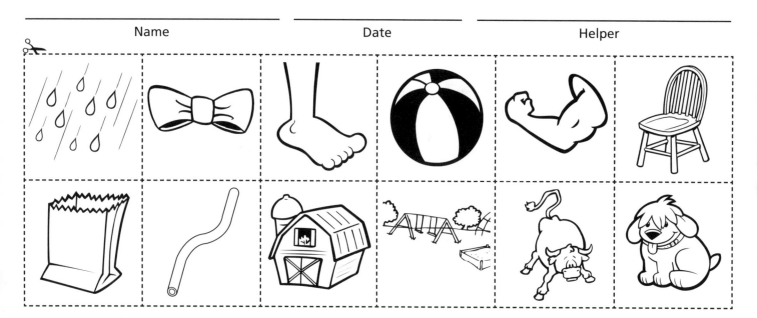

   **Segmentation**    #BK-330 Say & Glue® Phonological Awareness • ©2006 Super Duper® Publications • 1-800-277-8737 • www.superduperinc.com

# Segmentation Sensation

**Directions:** Cut along the dotted line and give the bottom sheet to the student. Have the student cut out the pictures. Helper says a compound word. The student says the two words that make up the word. The student finds the pictures for the compound word and glues/tapes or places them on the page.

**Teacher/Helper says:** **cowboy    cupcake    doorman    drumstick    earphone    eyeball**

✂

- - - - - - - - - - - - - - - - - - - - - - - - - - - - - - - - - - - - - - - - - - - - - - - - -

_____     _____     _____
Name                                               Date                                               Helper

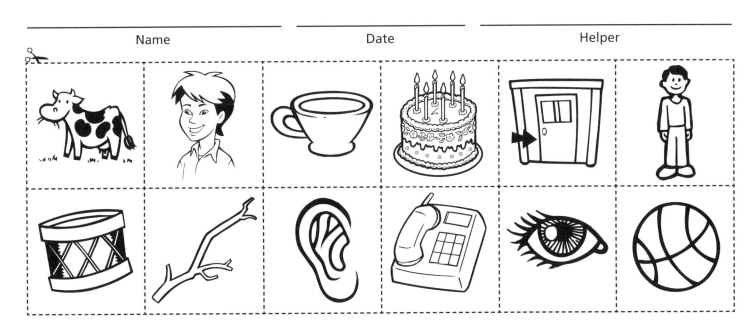

# Breakdown!

**Directions:** Cut along the dotted line and give the bottom sheet to the student. Have the student cut out the pictures. Helper says a compound word. The student says the two words that make up the word. The student finds the pictures for the compound word and glues/tapes or places them on the page.

**Teacher/Helper says:**  fingernail   fireman   hairbrush   honeybee   jellyfish   mailbox

Name _____  Date _____  Helper _____

Segmentation   #BK-330  Say & Glue® Phonological Awareness  •  ©2006 Super Duper® Publications  •  1-800-277-8737  •  www.superduperinc.com

# Word Attack!

**Directions:** Cut along the dotted line and give the bottom sheet to the student. Have the student cut out the pictures. Helper says a compound word. The student says the two words that make up the word. The student finds the pictures for the compound word and glues/tapes or places them on the page.

**Teacher/Helper says:**  fishbowl    handbag    keyhole    milkman    necktie    pancake

✂

_____  _____  _____
Name                                          Date                                        Helper

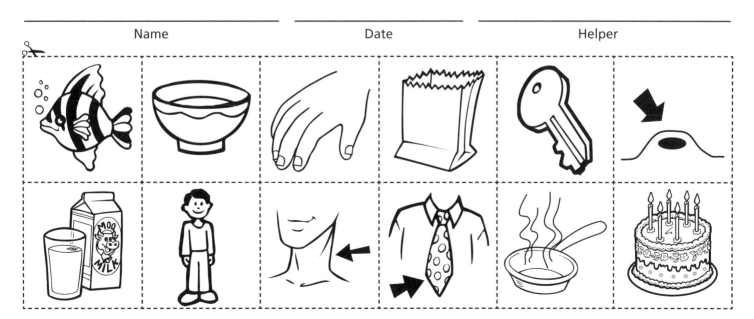

# Syllable Dribble

**Directions:** Cut along the dotted line and give the bottom sheet to the student. Have the student cut out the pictures. Helper says a compound word. The student says the two words that make up the word. The student finds the pictures for the compound word and glues/tapes or places them on the page.

**Teacher/Helper says:**   **flagpole   headdress   horsefly   houseboat   ladybug   stopwatch**

- - - - - - - - - - - - - - - - - - - - - - - - - - - - - - - - - - - - - - - - - - - - - ✂- - -

_____          _____          _____
Name                                            Date                                             Helper

Segmentation          #BK-330 Say & Glue® Phonological Awareness   •  ©2006 Super Duper® Publications  •  1-800-277-8737  •  www.superduperinc.com

# Superb Segmentation

**Directions:** Cut along the dotted line and give the bottom sheet to the student. Have the student cut out the pictures. Helper says a compound word. The student says the two words that make up the word. The student finds the pictures for the compound word and glues/tapes or places them on the page.

<u>**Teacher/Helper says:**</u>  **basketball   skateboard   snowman   hotdog   beanbag   catfish**

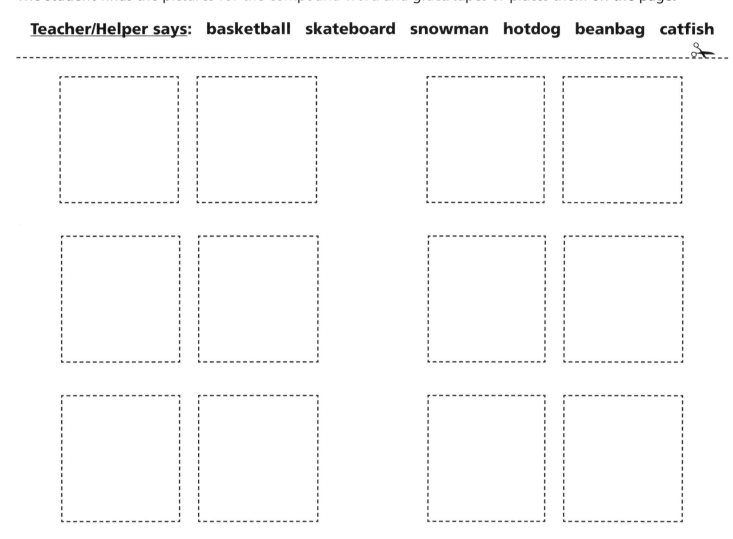

_____      _____      _____
Name                                         Date                                          Helper

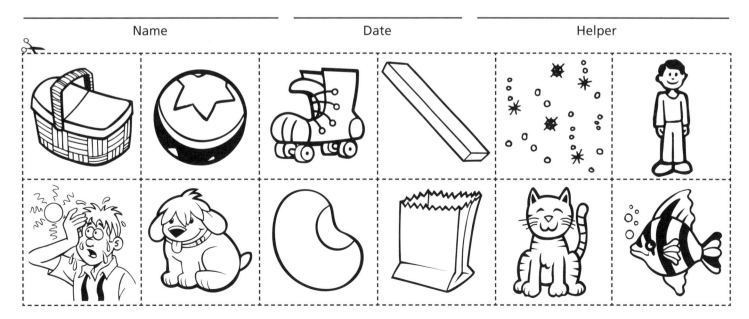

# Break It Up

**Directions:** Cut along the dotted line and give the bottom sheet to the student. Have the student cut out the pictures. Helper says a compound word. The student says the two words that make up the word. The student finds the pictures for the compound word and glues/tapes or places them on the page.

**Teacher/Helper says:** sandcastle   snowball   friendship   handshake   watermelon   backyard

✂ - - - - - - - - - - - - - - - - - - - - - - - - - - - - - - - - - - - - - - - - - - - - - - - - - - - -

| | | | |
|---|---|---|---|
| | | | |

| | | | |
|---|---|---|---|
| | | | |

| | | | |
|---|---|---|---|
| | | | |

_____     _____     _____
        Name                      Date                      Helper

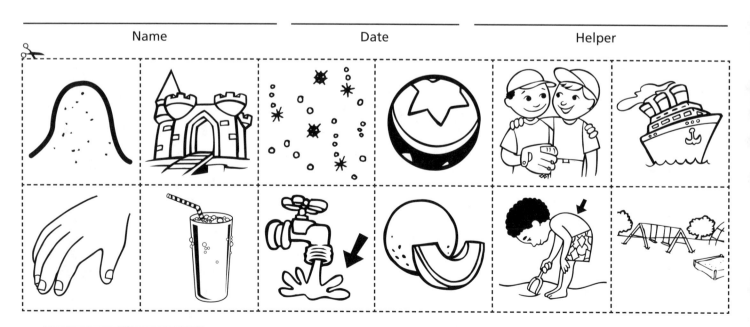

#BK-330 Say & Glue® Phonological Awareness • ©2006 Super Duper® Publications • 1-800-277-8737 • www.superduperinc.com

# Syllable Counting

 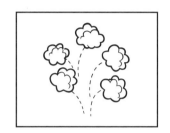  

  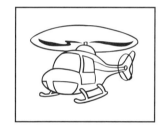 

 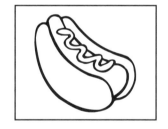  

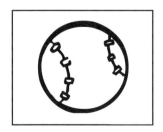   

# Syllable Countdown

**Directions:** Cut along the dotted line and give the bottom sheet to the student. Have the student cut out the pictures. Helper names each picture aloud. The student counts how many syllables (or parts of the word) it has by clapping or tapping. The student glues/tapes or places the picture on the side of the page matching that number of syllables in the word.

<u>**Teacher/Helper says**</u>**: How many syllables does the word _____ have?**

popcorn     fish     apple     pocket     dog     boat

- - - - - - - - - - - - - - - - - - - - - - - - - - - - - - - - - - - - - - - - - - - - - - - ✂

| | |
|:---:|:---:|
| **1** | **2** |

_____     _____     _____
Name                          Date                         Helper

  Syllable Counting          #BK-330 Say & Glue® Phonological Awareness • ©2006 Super Duper® Publications • 1-800-277-8737 • www.superduperinc.com

# Breakdown

**Directions:** Cut along the dotted line and give the bottom sheet to the student. Have the student cut out the pictures. Helper names each picture aloud. The student counts how many syllables (or parts of the word) it has by clapping or tapping. The student glues/tapes or places the picture on the side of the page matching that number of syllables in the word.

<u>**Teacher/Helper says:**</u> **How many syllables does the word _____ have?**

shoe      window      mailbox      book      car      mustard

| 1 | 2 |
|---|---|
|   |   |

_____      _____      _____
Name                    Date                    Helper

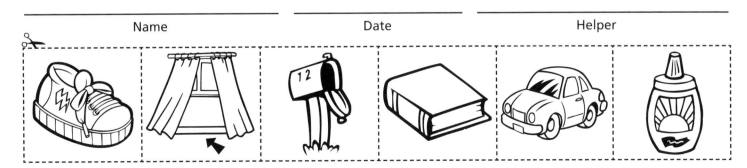

# Word Dissection

**Directions:** Cut along the dotted line and give the bottom sheet to the student. Have the student cut out the pictures. Helper names each picture aloud. The student counts how many syllables (or parts of the word) it has by clapping or tapping. The student glues/tapes or places the picture on the side of the page matching that number of syllables in the word.

<u>**Teacher/Helper says:**</u> **How many syllables does the word _____ have?**

bicycle      banana      cookie      sailboat      baseball      dinosaur

| 2 | 3 |
|---|---|
|   |   |

Name          Date          Helper

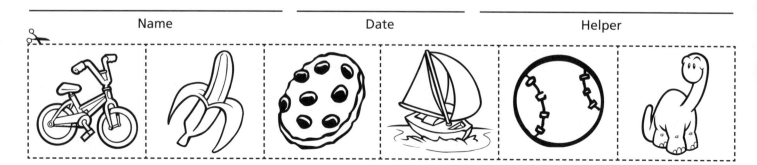

#BK-330 Say & Glue® Phonological Awareness • ©2006 Super Duper® Publications • 1-800-277-8737 • www.superduperinc.com

# Syllable Scouting

**Directions:** Cut along the dotted line and give the bottom sheet to the student. Have the student cut out the pictures. Helper names each picture aloud. The student counts how many syllables (or parts of the word) it has by clapping or tapping. The student glues/tapes or places the picture on the side of the page matching that number of syllables in the word.

<u>**Teacher/Helper says**</u>**: How many syllables does the word _____ have?**

| hamburger | bubble | water | potato | lemonade | money |

| 2 | 3 |
|---|---|
|   |   |

_____      _____      _____
Name                                          Date                                          Helper

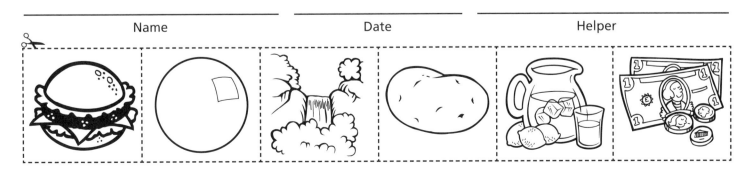

# Savvy Syllabification

**Directions:** Cut along the dotted line and give the bottom sheet to the student. Have the student cut out the pictures. Helper names each picture aloud. The student counts how many syllables (or parts of the word) it has by clapping or tapping. The student glues/tapes or places the picture on the side of the page matching that number of syllables in the word.

<u>**Teacher/Helper says:**</u> **How many syllables does the word _____ have?**

| bumblebee | helicopter | thermometer | elephant | telephone | dictionary |

- - - - - - - - - - - - - - - - - - - - - - - - - - - - - - - - - - - - - ✂ - - -

<table>
<tr><td>

# 3

</td><td>

# 4

</td></tr>
</table>

_____   _____   _____
Name                                    Date                                   Helper

✂ - - - - - - - - - - - - - - - - - - - - - - - - - - - - - - - - - - - - - - - - - -

Syllable Counting      #BK-330 Say & Glue® Phonological Awareness • ©2006 Super Duper® Publications • 1-800-277-8737 • www.superduperinc.com

# Count Those Syllables!

**Directions:** Cut along the dotted line and give the bottom sheet to the student. Have the student cut out the pictures. Helper names each picture aloud. The student counts how many syllables (or parts of the word) it has by clapping or tapping. The student glues/tapes or places the picture on the side of the page matching that number of syllables in the word.

**Teacher/Helper says: How many syllables does the word _____ have?**

computer        calculator        sunflower        television        umbrella        alligator

- - - - - - - - - - - - - - - - - - - - - - - - - - - - - - - - - - - - - - - - - - - - - ✂

| 3 | 4 |
|---|---|
|   |   |

_____        _____        _____
Name                                      Date                                        Helper

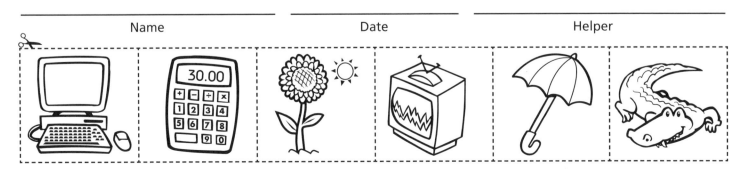

# Break It Down!

**Directions:** Cut along the dotted line and give the bottom sheet to the student.  Have the student cut out the pictures.  Helper names each picture aloud.  The student counts how many syllables (or parts of the word) it has by clapping or tapping.  The student glues/tapes or places the picture on the side of the page matching that number of syllables in the word.

**Teacher/Helper says: How many syllables does the word _____ have?**

radio          celebration          cantaloupe          tarantula          cheerleader          medication

- - - - - - - - - - - - - - - - - - - - - - - - - - - - - - - - - - - - - - - - - - - - - - - - - ✂ - - - - -

| 3 | 4 |
|---|---|
|   |   |

_____    _____    _____
Name                                        Date                                         Helper

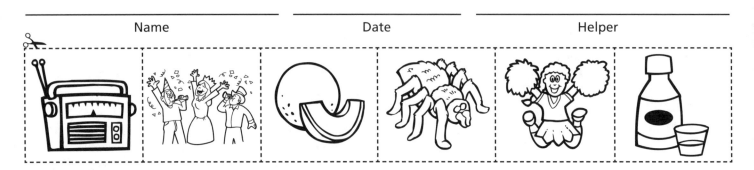

 Syllable Counting          #BK-330  Say & Glue® Phonological Awareness  •  ©2006 Super Duper® Publications  •  1-800-277-8737  •  www.superduperinc.com

# Letter Sounds

   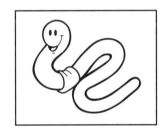

   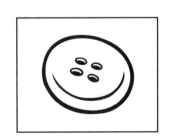

# Letter Limbo - Beginning

**Directions:** Cut along the dotted line and give the bottom sheet to the student. Have the student cut out the pictures. Helper names a picture aloud. The student finds the picture and glues/tapes or places it on the letter box that has the same <u>beginning</u> sound *(pear, puzzle, peanut, mouse, mop, money, teacher, teeth, table, sandwich, saw, seal)*.

| | |
|:---:|:---:|
| P | M |
| T | S |

Name         Date         Helper

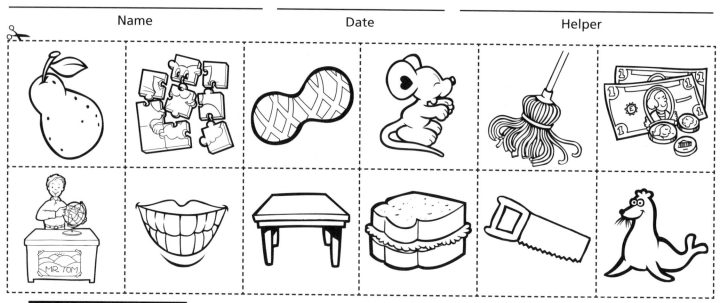

 #BK-330 Say & Glue® Phonological Awareness   ©2006 Super Duper® Publications • 1-800-277-8737 • www.superduperinc.com

# Sound Surprise - Beginning

**Directions:** Cut along the dotted line and give the bottom sheet to the student. Have the student cut out the pictures. Helper names a picture aloud. The student finds the picture and glues/tapes or places it on the letter box that has the same <u>beginning</u> sound *(ball, bottle, bell, rock, rake, rattle, kite, key, kitten, wagon, wheel, web).*

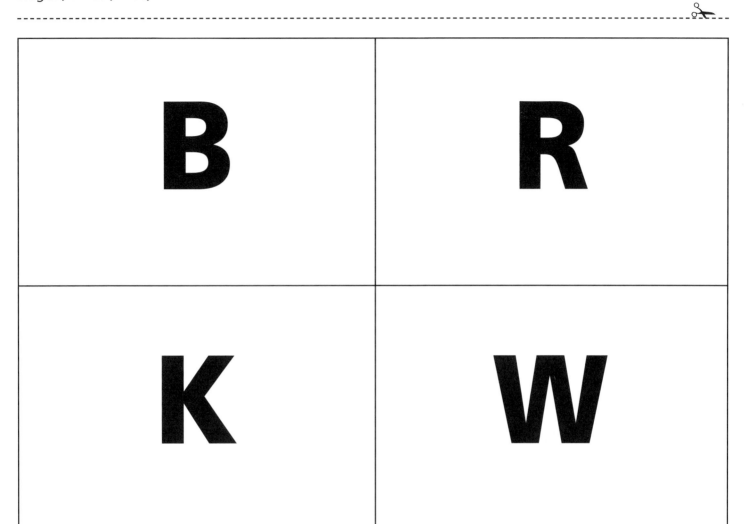

Name          Date          Helper

# Magic Match-Up - Beginning

**Directions:** Cut along the dotted line and give the bottom sheet to the student. Have the student cut out the pictures. Helper names a picture aloud. The student finds the picture and glues/tapes or places it on the letter box that has the same <u>beginning</u> sound *(diamond, daisy, donut, fish, five, fan, girl, ghost, gift, hammer, hamburger, hand)*.

| | |
|:---:|:---:|
| **D** | **F** |
| **G** | **H** |

Name      Date      Helper

 #BK-330 Say & Glue® Phonological Awareness • ©2006 Super Duper® Publications • 1-800-277-8737 • www.superduperinc.com

# Say It, Paste It - Beginning

**Directions:** Cut along the dotted line and give the bottom sheet to the student. Have the student cut out the pictures. Helper names a picture aloud. The student finds the picture and glues/tapes or places it on the letter box that has the same <u>beginning</u> sound *(needle, nail, nest, vest, violin, van, jar, jet, jaw, cup, cone, coat).*

✂ - - - - - - - - - - - - - - - - - - - - - - - - - - - - - - - - - - - - - - - - - - - - - - - - - - - - - - - - - -

| | |
|:---:|:---:|
| **N** | **V** |
| **J** | **C** |

_____  _____  _____
Name              Date              Helper

# Vowel Power - Beginning

**Directions:** Cut along the dotted line and give bottom sheet to the student. Have the student cut out the pictures. Helper names a picture aloud. The student finds the picture and glues/tapes or places it on the letter box that has the same <u>beginning</u> sound *(apple, alligator, ax, elbow, egg, elephant, igloo, inch, itch, octopus, ostrich, out).*

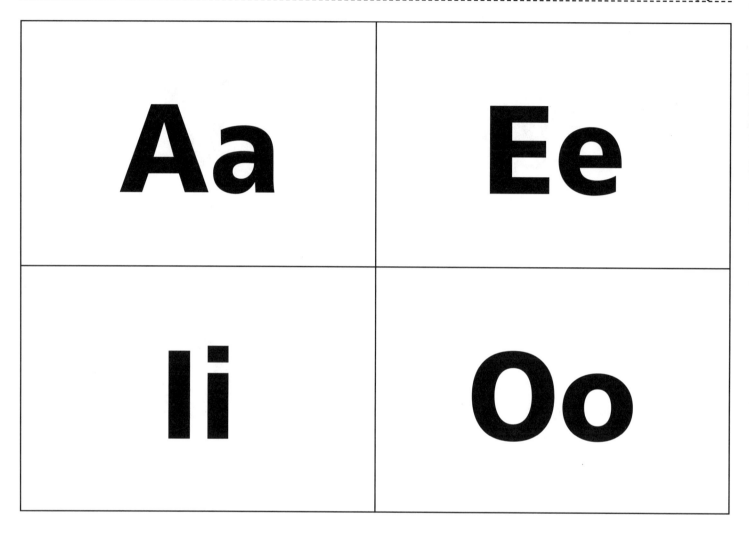

Name          Date          Helper

 Beginning Letter Sounds          #BK-330 Say & Glue® Phonological Awareness · ©2006 Super Duper® Publications · 1-800-277-8737 · www.superduperinc.com

# Sensational Sounds - Beginning

**Directions:** Cut along the dotted line and give the bottom sheet to the student. Have the student cut out the pictures. Helper names a picture aloud. The student finds the picture and glues/tapes or places it on the letter box that has the same <u>beginning</u> sound *(yarn, yo-yo, yard, umbrella, upset, under, leg, lamp, laces, question, quarter, queen).*

| | |
|---|---|
| **Y** | **U** |
| **L** | **Q** |

_____   _____   _____
Name                          Date                           Helper

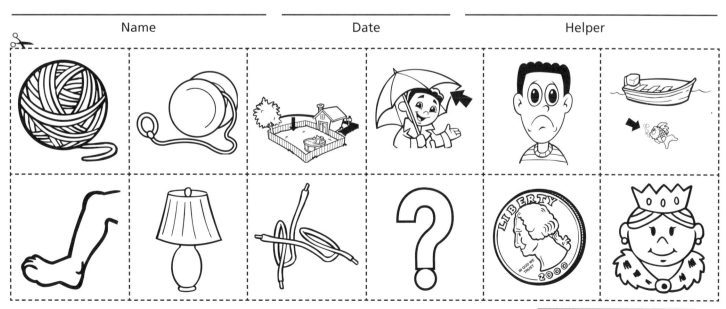

# Letter Limbo - Ending

**Directions:** Cut along the dotted line and give the bottom sheet to the student. Have the student cut out the pictures. Helper names a picture aloud. The student finds the picture and glues/tapes or places it on the letter box that has the same <u>ending</u> sound *(bowl, eel, mail, fence, purse, pearls, broom, comb, ice cream, boat, boot, hat)*.

✂

| | |
|:---:|:---:|
| **L** | **S** |
| **M** | **T** |

| | | |
|---|---|---|
| Name | Date | Helper |

✂

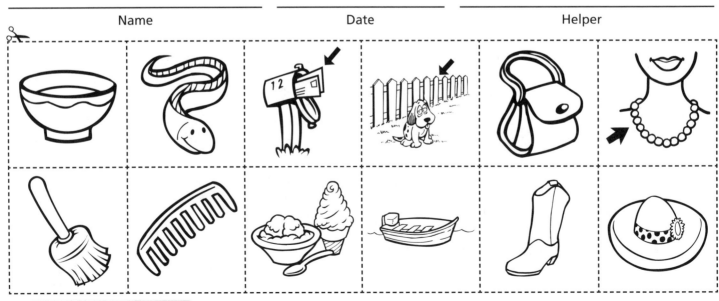

**Ending Letter Sounds**  #BK-330 Say & Glue® Phonological Awareness • ©2006 Super Duper® Publications • 1-800-277-8737 • www.superduperinc.com

# Sound Surprise - Ending

**Directions:** Cut along the dotted line and give the bottom sheet to the student. Have the student cut out the pictures. Helper names a picture aloud. The student finds the picture and glues/tapes or places it on the letter box that has the same <u>ending</u> sound *(knob, cab, crab, drum, jam, worm, lettuce, cactus, birdhouse, knife, loaf, roof)*.

| | |
|---|---|
| **B** | **M** |
| **S** | **F** |

_____    _____    _____
Name                                        Date                                          Helper

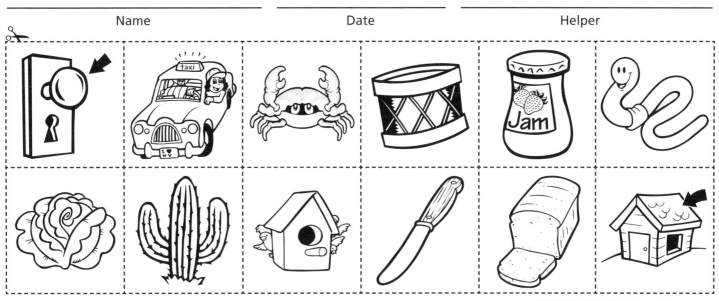

# Magic Match-Up - Ending

**Directions:** Cut along the dotted line and give the bottom sheet to the student. Have the student cut out the pictures. Helper names a picture aloud. The student finds the picture and glues/tapes or places it on the letter box that has the same <u>ending</u> sound *(dice, dress, mouse, wrist, donut, cot, crib, web, bib, snake, sock, block).*

✂ - - - - - - - - - - - - - - - - - - - - - - - - - - - - - - - - - - - - - - - - -

| | |
|:---:|:---:|
| **S** | **T** |
| **B** | **K** |

| Name | Date | Helper |
|---|---|---|

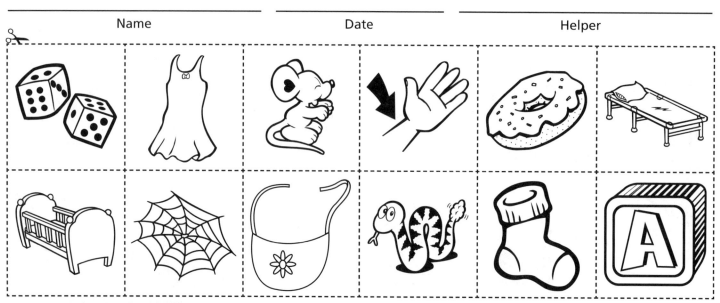

 **Ending Letter Sounds**    #BK-330 Say & Glue® Phonological Awareness  •  ©2006 Super Duper® Publications  •  1-800-277-8737  •  www.superduperinc.com

# Say It, Paste It - Ending

**Directions:** Cut along the dotted line and give the bottom sheet to the student. Have the student cut out the pictures. Helper names a picture aloud. The student finds the picture and glues/tapes or places it on the letter box that has the same <u>ending</u> sound *(lamb, home, game, bed, sand, hand, rug, bag, flag, tulip, rope, soup).*

| | |
|:---:|:---:|
| **M** | **D** |
| **G** | **P** |

_____  _____  _____
Name                              Date                              Helper

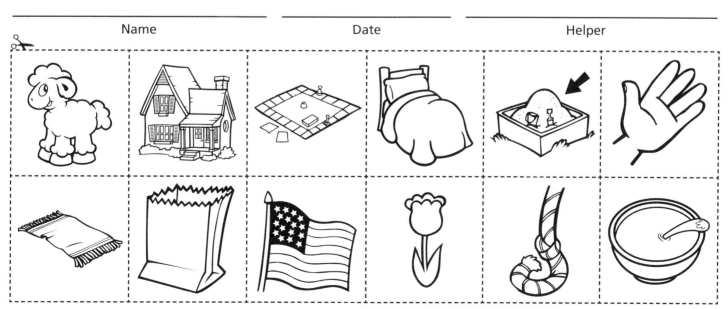

# Sensational Sounds - Ending

**Directions:** Cut along the dotted line and give the bottom sheet to the student. Have the student cut out the pictures. Helper names a picture aloud. The student finds the picture and glues/tapes or places it on the letter box that has the same <u>ending</u> sound (*leaf, cuff, golf, heel, snail, whale, spoon, phone, balloon, glove, hive, five*).

✂ - - - - - - - - - - - - - - - - - - - - - - - - - - - - - - - - - - - - - - - - - - - - - - - - - - - - - - - - - - - - - -

| | |
|:---:|:---:|
| **F** | **L** |
| **N** | **V** |

| | | |
|:---:|:---:|:---:|
| Name | Date | Helper |

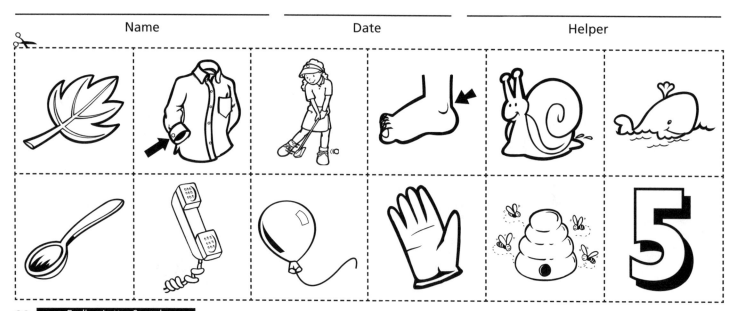

#BK-330  Say & Glue® Phonological Awareness • ©2006 Super Duper® Publications • 1-800-277-8737 • www.superduperinc.com

# Name Game - Beginning

**Directions:** Cut along the dotted line and give the bottom sheet to the student. Have the student cut out the pictures. Helper names a picture aloud. The student finds the picture and glues/tapes or places it with the person whose name has the same <u>beginning</u> sound *(marshmallows, mouse, mail, door, dish, doll, button, box, beard, pencil, peach, pearls).*

✂ - - - - - - - - - - - - - - - - - - - - - - - - - - - - - - - - - - - - - - - - - - - - - - - - - - - - - - - - - - -

**Mary**

**David**

**Bob**

**Paula**

_____    _____    _____
Name                        Date                        Helper

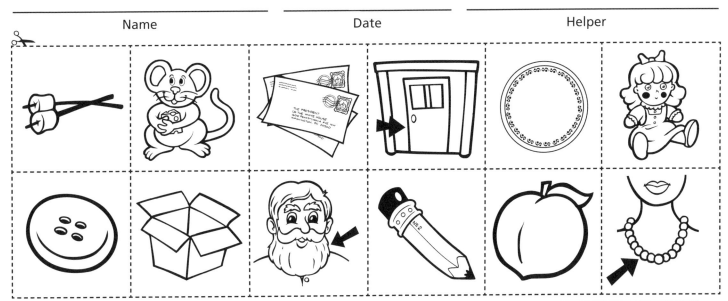

# It's All in a Name - Beginning

**Directions:** Cut along the dotted line and give the bottom sheet to the student. Have the student cut out the pictures. Helper names a picture aloud. The student finds the picture and glues/tapes or places it with the person whose name has the same <u>beginning</u> sound *(apple, alligator, axe, jet, jellyfish, jewels, rope, rock, ring, egg, elephant, elf).*

- - - - - - - - - - - - - - - - - - - - - - - - - - - - - - - - - - - - - - - - - - - - - - - - - - - - ✂

| | |
|---|---|
| **Abby** | **Jill** |
| **Robert** | **Evan** |

_____  _____  _____
Name                          Date                          Helper

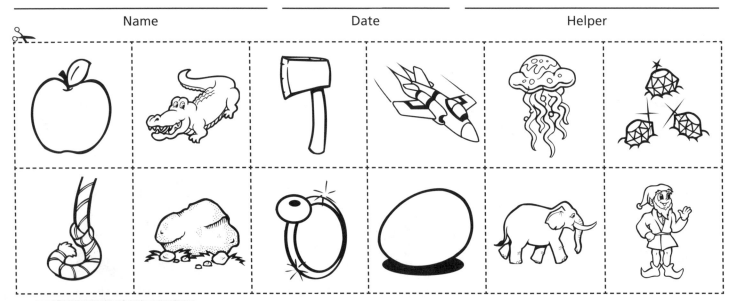

#BK-330 Say & Glue® Phonological Awareness • ©2006 Super Duper® Publications • 1-800-277-8737 • www.superduperinc.com

# Sounds Like - Beginning

**Directions:** Cut along the dotted line and give the bottom sheet to the student. Have the student cut out the pictures. Helper names a picture aloud. The student finds the picture and glues/tapes or places it with the person whose name has the same <u>beginning</u> sound (*teeth, teepee, taco, lemon, lamp, limb, kangaroo, king, kite, nails, numbers, newspaper*).

Name _____  Date _____  Helper _____

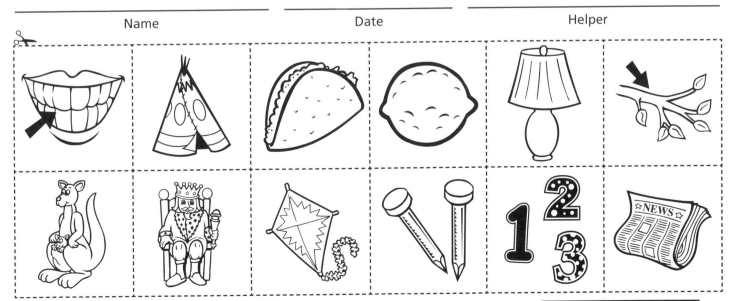

# Fun With Names - Beginning

**Directions:** Cut along the dotted line and give the bottom sheet to the student. Have the student cut out the pictures. Helper names a picture aloud. The student finds the picture and glues/tapes or places it with the person whose name has the same <u>beginning</u> sound (*inch, igloo, ill, seventeen, salt, sunflower, window, wand, whale, zero, zipper, zucchini*).

Name _____  Date _____  Helper _____

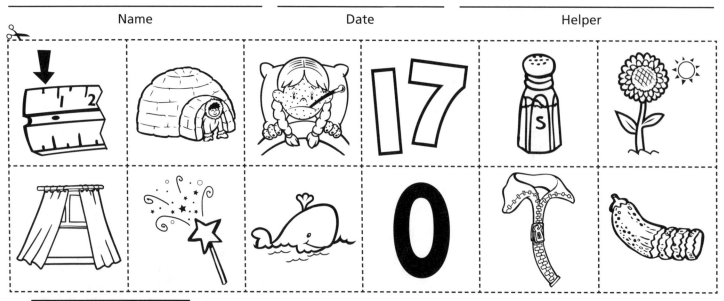

 Beginning Letter Sounds    #BK-330 *Say & Glue®* Phonological Awareness • ©2006 Super Duper® Publications • 1-800-277-8737 • www.superduperinc.com

# Notable Names - Beginning

**Directions:** Cut along the dotted line and give the bottom sheet to the student. Have the student cut out the pictures. Helper names a picture aloud. The student finds the picture and glues/tapes or places it with the person whose name has the same <u>beginning</u> sound *(ape, acorn, apron, open, oak, ocean, hoe, hop, helmet, feather, fireworks, four).*

| Name | Date | Helper |

# People Pleasers - Beginning

**Directions:** Cut along the dotted line and give the bottom sheet to the student. Have the student cut out the pictures. Helper names a picture aloud. The student finds the picture and glues/tapes or places it with the person whose name has the same <u>beginning</u> sound *(ice cream, eye, iron, eat, ear, eel, violin, vase, vegetables, cookie, cat, cup).*

Name _____  Date _____  Helper _____

 **Beginning Letter Sounds** #BK-330 *Say & Glue® Phonological Awareness* • ©2006 Super Duper® Publications • 1-800-277-8737 • www.superduperinc.com

# Syllable/Phoneme Deletion

# Around the House

**Directions:** Cut along the dotted line and give the bottom sheet to the student. Have the student cut out the pictures. Helper reads the clues below, and the student says the new word. Student finds the picture that matches the new word and glues/tapes or places it on the scene.

1. Say **doghouse**. Now say it without **house**. *(dog)*
2. Say **bedroom**. Now say it without **room**. *(bed)*
3. Say **mailman**. Now say it without **man**. *(mail)*
4. Say **toothbrush**. Now say it without **tooth**. *(brush)*
5. Say **horseshoe**. Now say it without **horse**. *(shoe)*
6. Say **pancake**. Now say it without **cake**. *(pan)*

Name           Date           Helper

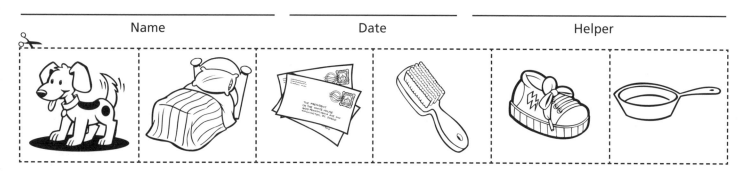

Syllable/Phoneme Deletion    #BK-330 Say & Glue® Phonological Awareness • ©2006 Super Duper® Publications • 1-800-277-8737 • www.superduperinc.com

# At the Beach

**Directions:** Cut along the dotted line and give the bottom sheet to the student. Have the student cut out the pictures. Helper reads the clues below, and the student says the new word. Student finds the picture that matches the new word and glues/tapes or places it on the scene.

1. Say **seashell**. Now say it without **sea**. *(shell)*
2. Say **parasail**. Now say it without **para**. *(sail)*
3. Say **frisbee**. Now say it without **fris**. *(bee)*
4. Say **jellyfish**. Now say it without **jelly**. *(fish)*
5. Say **rowboat**. Now say it without **row**. *(boat)*
6. Say **dolphin**. Now say it without **dol**. *(phin)*

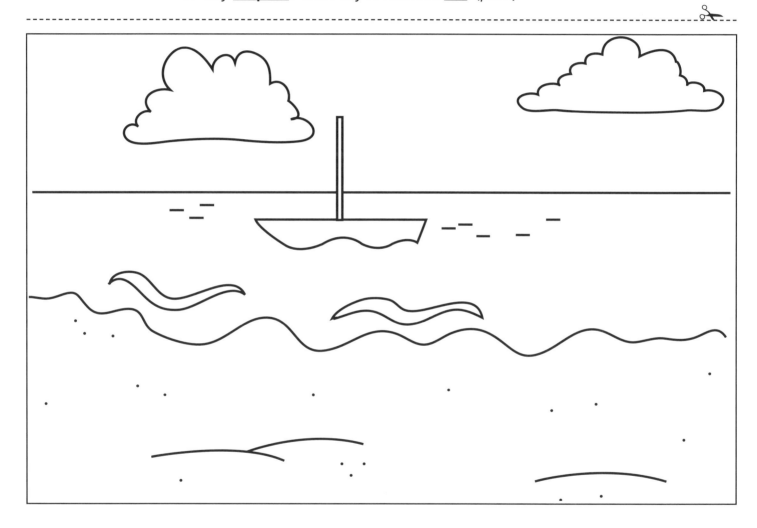

Name _____  Date _____  Helper _____

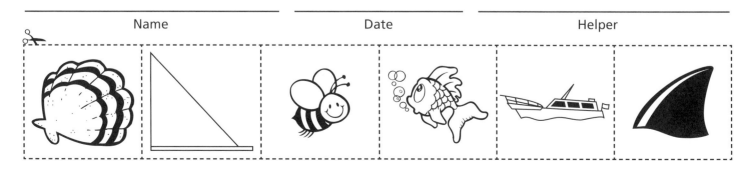

# The Store

**Directions:** Cut along the dotted line and give the bottom sheet to the student. Have the student cut out the pictures. Helper reads the clues below, and the student says the new word. Student finds the picture that matches the new word and glues/tapes or places it on the scene.

1. Say **airplane**. Now say it without **air**. *(plane)*
2. Say **doughnuts**. Now say it without **dough**. *(nuts)*
3. Say **popcorn**. Now say it without **pop**. *(corn)*
4. Say **baseball**. Now say it without **base**. *(ball)*
5. Say **mailbox**. Now say it without **mail**. *(box)*
6. Say **grapefruit**. Now say it without **grape**. *(fruit)*

Name        Date        Helper

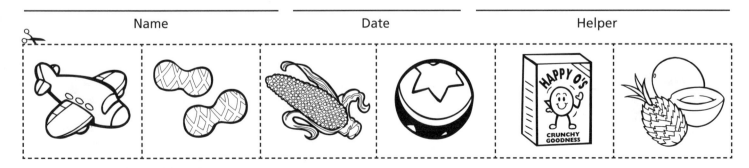

 **Syllable/Phoneme Deletion**    #BK-330 Say & Glue® Phonological Awareness • ©2006 Super Duper® Publications • 1-800-277-8737 • www.superduperinc.com

# On the Farm

**Directions:** Cut along the dotted line and give the bottom sheet to the student. Have the student cut out the pictures. Helper reads the clues below, and the student says the new word. Student finds the picture that matches the new word and glues/tapes or places it on the scene.

1. Say **mousetrap**. Now say it without **trap**. *(mouse)*
2. Say **birdhouse**. Now say it without **house**. *(bird)*
3. Say **cowboy**. Now say it without **boy**. *(cow)*
4. Say **grasshopper**. Now say it without **hopper**. *(grass)*
5. Say **sailboat**. Now say it without **sail**. *(boat)*
6. Say **boyfriend**. Now say it without **friend**. *(boy)*

Name        Date        Helper

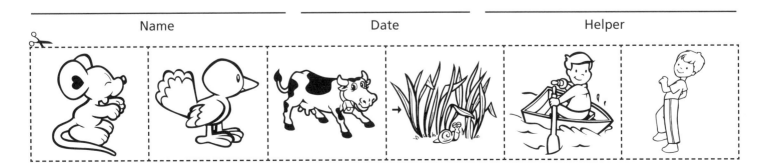

# Soccer Game

**Directions:** Cut along the dotted line and give the bottom sheet to the student. Have the student cut out the pictures. Helper reads the directions below, and the student follows them. After the student finishes, he/she glues/tapes or places the picture on the scene.

1. Find the ball. Say **ball**. Now say it without "**b**." *(all)*

2. Find the cleat. Say **cleat**. Now say it without "**c**." *(leat)*

3. Find the goal. Say **goal**. Now say it without "**g**." *(oal)*

4. Find the bottle. Say **bottle**. Now say it without "**bo**." *(ttle)*

5. Find the chair. Say **chair**. Now say it without "**ch**." *(air)*

6. Find the coach. Say **coach**. Now say it without "**c**." *(oach)*

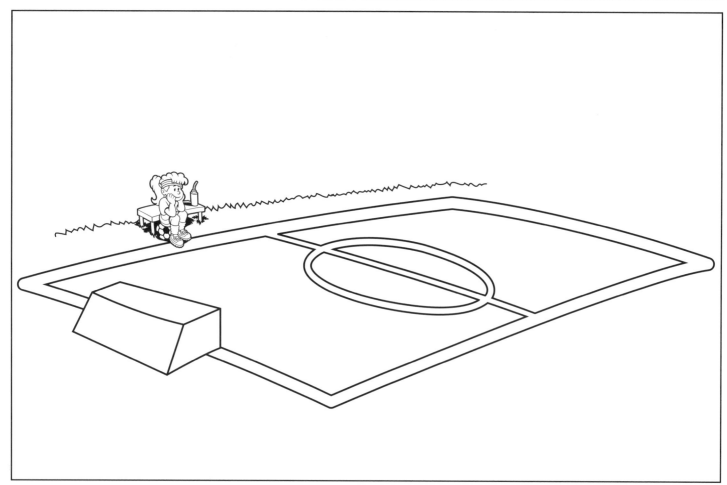

Name _____  Date _____  Helper _____

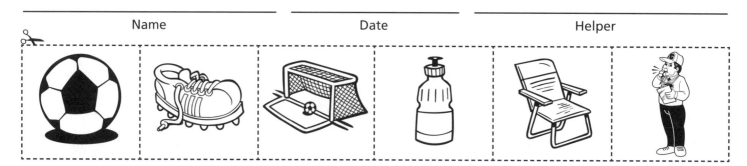

#BK-330 Say & Glue® Phonological Awareness • ©2006 Super Duper® Publications • 1-800-277-8737 • www.superduperinc.com

# Bike Shop

**Directions:** Cut along the dotted line and give the bottom sheet to the student. Have the student cut out the pictures. Helper reads the directions below, and the student follows them. After the student finishes, he/she glues/tapes or places the picture on the scene.

1. Find the pedal. Say **pedal**. Now say it without "**dal**." *(pe)*

2. Find the seat. Say **seat**. Now say it without "**t**." *(sea)*

3. Find the money. Say **money**. Now say it without "**ney**." *(mo)*

4. Find the bell. Say **bell**. Now say it without "**ell**." *(b)*

5. Find the basket. Say **basket**. Now say it without "**et**." *(bask)*

6. Find the tire. Say **tire**. Now say it without "**r**." *(ti)*

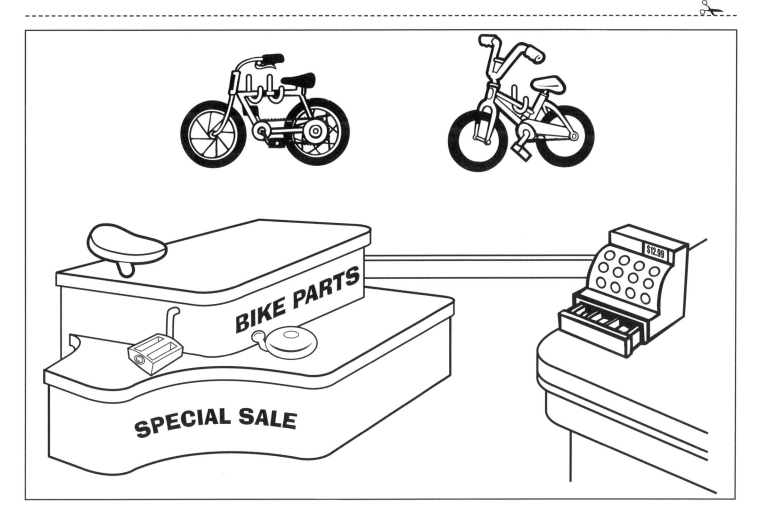

Name          Date          Helper

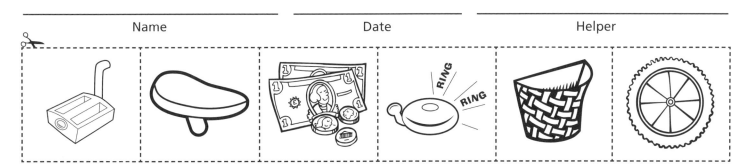

# Clothing Store

**Directions:** Cut along the dotted line and give the bottom sheet to the student. Have the student cut out the pictures. Helper reads the directions below, and the student follows them. After the student finishes, he/she glues/tapes or places the picture on the scene.

1. Find the shoes. Say **shoes**. Now say it without "**oes**." (sh)
2. Find the shirt. Say **shirt**. Now say it without "**t**." (shir)
3. Find the coat. Say **coat**. Now say it without "**t**." (coa)
4. Find the hat. Say **hat**. Now say it without "**t**." (ha)
5. Find the socks. Say **socks**. Now say it without "**ks**." (so)
6. Find the pants. Say **pants**. Now say it without "**s**." (pant)

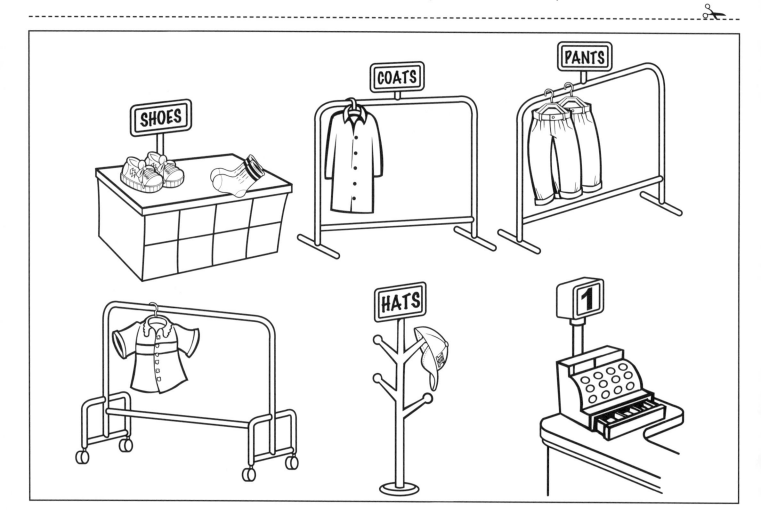

| Name | Date | Helper |

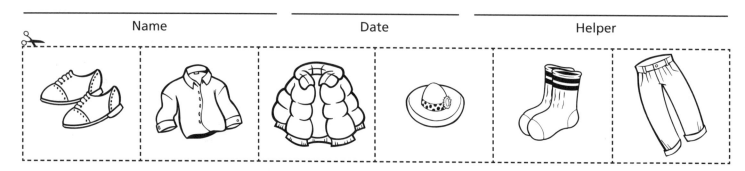

 #BK-330 Say & Glue® Phonological Awareness • ©2006 Super Duper® Publications • 1-800-277-8737 • www.superduperinc.com

# City Park

**Directions:** Cut along the dotted line and give the bottom sheet to the student. Have the student cut out the pictures. Helper reads the directions below, and the student follows them. After the student finishes, he/she glues/tapes or places the picture on the scene.

1. Find the dog. Say **dog**. Now say it without "**g**." *(do)*
2. Find the ball. Say **ball**. Now say it without "**all**." *(b)*
3. Find the boy. Say **boy**. Now say it without "**oy**." *(b)*
4. Find the bat. Say **bat**. Now say it without "**t**." *(ba)*
5. Find the girl. Say **girl**. Now say it without "**l**." *(gir)*
6. Find the bike. Say **bike**. Now say it without "**ke**." *(bi)*

Name        Date        Helper

# In the Bedroom

**Directions:** Cut along the dotted line and give the bottom sheet to the student. Have the student cut out the pictures. Helper reads the directions below, and the student follows them. After the student finishes, he/she glues/tapes or places the picture on the scene.

1. Find the pillow. Say **pillow**. Now say it without "**ow**." *(pill)*
2. Find the window. Say **window**. Now say it without "**ow**." *(wind)*
3. Find the shirt. Say **shirt**. Now say it without "**t**." *(shir)*
4. Find the shoe. Say **shoe**. Now say it without "**oe**." *(sh)*
5. Find the book. Say **book**. Now say it without "**k**." *(boo)*
6. Find the hat. Say **hat**. Now say it without "**t**." *(ha)*

| Name | Date | Helper |
|---|---|---|

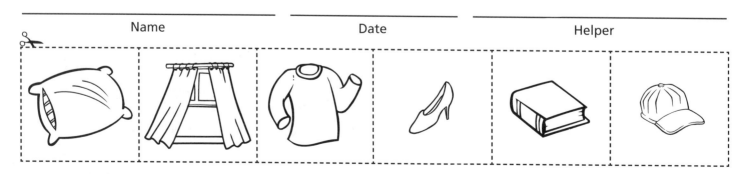

 Syllable/Phoneme Deletion     #BK-330  Say & Glue® Phonological Awareness • ©2006 Super Duper® Publications • 1-800-277-8737 • www.superduperinc.com

# Syllable/Phoneme Addition

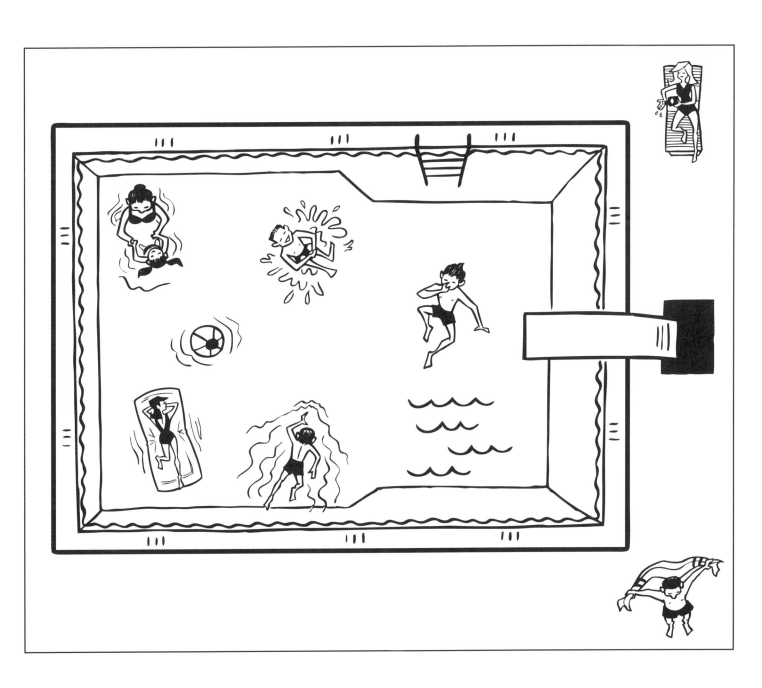

# At the Diner

**Directions:** Cut along the dotted line and give the bottom sheet to the student. Have the student cut out the pictures. Helper reads the clues below, and the student says the new word. The student finds the picture that matches the new word and glues/tapes or places it on the scene.

1. Say <u>dough</u>. Now say it with <u>nut</u> at the end. (*doughnut*)
2. Say <u>milk</u>. Now say it with <u>shake</u> at the end. (*milkshake*)
3. Say <u>oat</u>. Now say it with <u>meal</u> at the end. (*oatmeal*)
4. Say <u>pan</u>. Now say it with <u>cake</u> at the end. (*pancake*)
5. Say <u>pea</u>. Now say it with <u>nut</u> at the end. (*peanut*)
6. Say <u>pop</u>. Now say it with <u>corn</u> at the end. (*popcorn*)

Name          Date          Helper

Syllable/Phoneme Addition   #BK-330 Say & Glue® Phonological Awareness • ©2006 Super Duper® Publications • 1-800-277-8737 • www.superduperinc.com

# Dress-Up

**Directions:** Cut along the dotted line and give the bottom sheet to the student. Have the student cut out the pictures. Helper reads the clues below, and the student says the new word. The student finds the picture that matches the new word and glues/tapes or places it on the scene.

1. Say <u>eye</u>. Now say it with <u>lash</u> at the end. *(eyelash)*
2. Say <u>brace</u>. Now say it with <u>let</u> at the end. *(bracelet)*
3. Say <u>neck</u>. Now say it with <u>lace</u> at the end. *(necklace)*
4. Say <u>wrist</u>. Now say it with <u>watch</u> at the end. *(wristwatch)*
5. Say <u>hair</u>. Now say it with <u>bow</u> at the end. *(hairbow)*
6. Say <u>ear</u>. Now say it with <u>ring</u> at the end. *(earring)*

| Name | Date | Helper |
|------|------|--------|

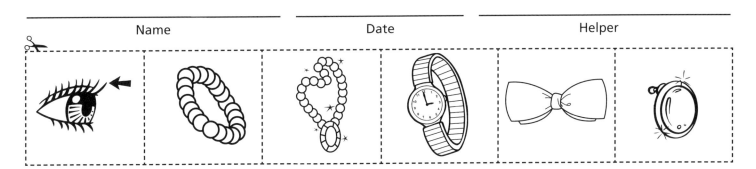

#BK-330 Say & Glue® Phonological Awareness • ©2006 Super Duper® Publications • 1-800-277-8737 • www.superduperinc.com

# Football Game

**Directions:** Cut along the dotted line and give the bottom sheet to the student.  Have the student cut out the pictures.  Helper reads the clues below, and the student says the new word.  The student finds the picture that matches the new word and glues/tapes or places it on the scene.

1. Say **touch**.  Now say it with **down** at the end. *(touchdown)*
2. Say **foot**.  Now say it with **ball** at the end. *(football)*
3. Say **kick**.  Now say it with **off** at the end. *(kickoff)*
4. Say **quarter**.  Now say it with **back** at the end. *(quarterback)*
5. Say **team**.  Now say it with **mate** at the end. *(teammate)*
6. Say **cheer**.  Now say it with **leader** at the end. *(cheerleader)*

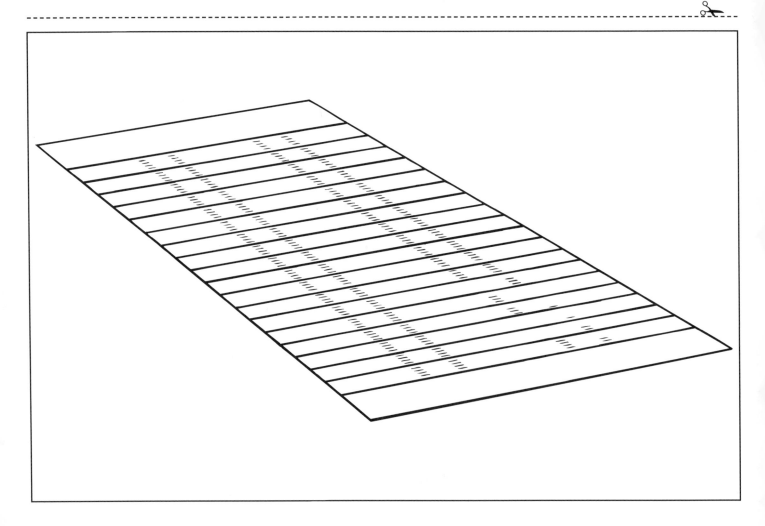

_____   _____   _____
Name                                   Date                                   Helper

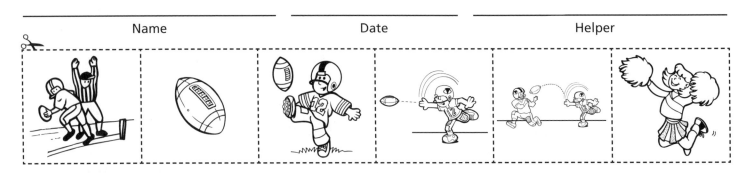

 Syllable/Phoneme Addition    #BK-330 Say & Glue® Phonological Awareness  •  ©2006 Super Duper® Publications  •  1-800-277-8737  •  www.superduperinc.com

# Dog Wash

**Directions:** Cut along the dotted line and give the bottom sheet to the student. Have the student cut out the pictures. Helper reads the clues below, and the student says the new word. The student finds the picture that matches the new word and glues/tapes or places it on the scene.

1. Say "**wa**." Now say it with "**ter**" at the end. *(water)*
2. Say "**s**." Now say it with "**oap**" at the end. *(soap)*
3. Say "**do**." Now say it with "**g**" at the end. *(dog)*
4. Say "**tu**." Now say it with "**b**" at the end. *(tub)*
5. Say "**tow**." Now say it with "**el**" at the end. *(towel)*
6. Say "**spl**." Now say it with "**ash**" at the end. *(splash)*

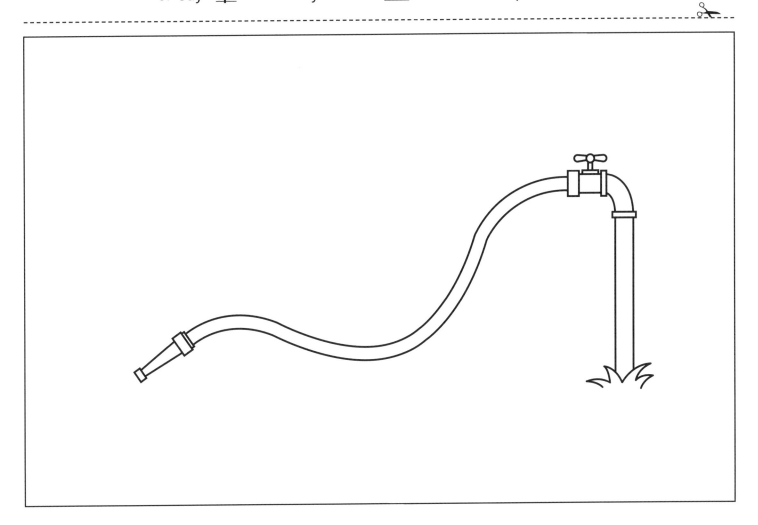

Name _____   Date _____   Helper _____

# Nighttime

**Directions:** Cut along the dotted line and give the bottom sheet to the student. Have the student cut out the pictures. Helper reads the clues below, and the student says the new word. The student finds the picture that matches the new word and glues/tapes or places it on the scene.

1. Say "<u>st</u>." Now say it with "<u>ar</u>" at the end. *(star)*

2. Say "<u>moo</u>." Now say it with "<u>n</u>" at the end. *(moon)*

3. Say "<u>ten</u>." Now say it with "<u>t</u>" at the end. *(tent)*

4. Say "<u>twin</u>." Now say it with "<u>kle</u>" at the end. *(twinkle)*

5. Say "<u>flash</u>." Now say it with "<u>light</u>" at the end. *(flashlight)*

6. Say "<u>fire</u>." Now say it with "<u>fly</u>" at the end. *(firefly)*

| Name | Date | Helper |
|------|------|--------|

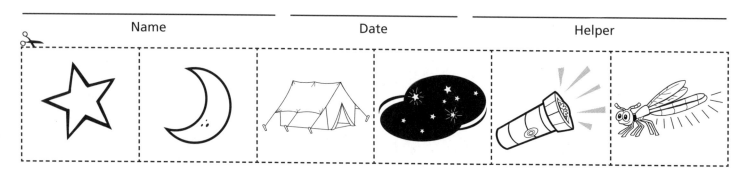

 Syllable/Phoneme Addition    #BK-330 Say & Glue® Phonological Awareness • ©2006 Super Duper® Publications • 1-800-277-8737 • www.superduperinc.com

# Movie Night

**Directions:** Cut along the dotted line and give the bottom sheet to the student. Have the student cut out the pictures. Helper reads the clues below, and the student says the new word. The student finds the picture that matches the new word and glues/tapes or places it on the scene.

1. Say "**pop**." Now say it with "**ping**" at the end. *(popping)*
2. Say "**sal**." Now say it with "**ty**" at the end. *(salty)*
3. Say "**but**." Now say it with "**ter**" at the end. *(butter)*
4. Say "**buc**." Now say it with "**ket**" at the end. *(bucket)*
5. Say "**eat**." Now say it with "**ing**" at the end. *(eating)*
6. Say "**can**." Now say it with "**dy**" at the end. *(candy)*

Name       Date       Helper

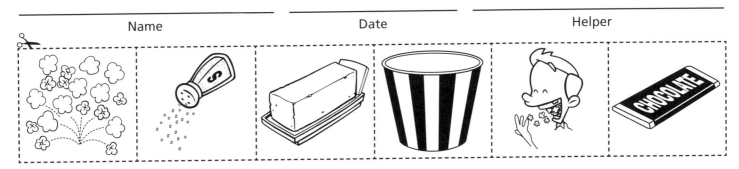

# At the Pool

**Directions:** Cut along the dotted line and give the bottom sheet to the student. Have the student cut out the pictures. Helper reads the clues below, and the student says the new word. The student finds the picture that matches the new word and glues/tapes or places it on the scene.

1. Say "<u>fl</u>." Now say it with "<u>oat</u>" at the end. *(float)*
2. Say "<u>wa</u>." Now say it with "<u>ter</u>" at the end. *(water)*
3. Say "<u>spla</u>." Now say it with "<u>sh</u>" at the end. *(splash)*
4. Say "<u>j</u>." Now say it with "<u>ump</u>" at the end. *(jump)*
5. Say "<u>lo</u>." Now say it with "<u>tion</u>" at the end. *(lotion)*
6. Say "<u>tow</u>." Now say it with "<u>el</u>" at the end. *(towel)*

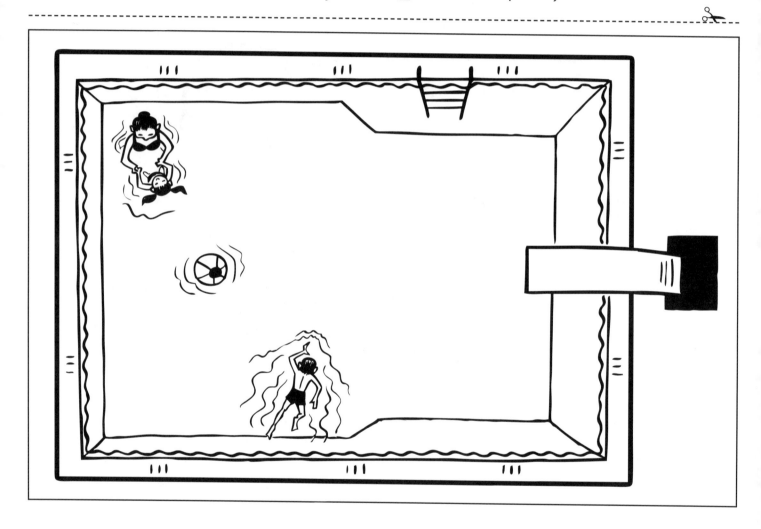

Name      Date      Helper

 #BK-330 Say & Glue® Phonological Awareness • ©2006 Super Duper® Publications • 1-800-277-8737 • www.superduperinc.com

# Manipulation of Phonemes

  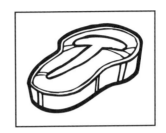 

   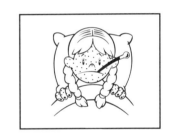

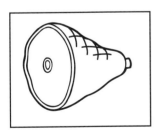 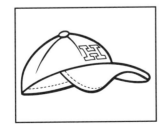  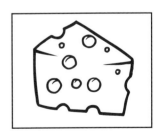

# Down with Sounds

**Directions:** Cut along the dotted line and give the bottom sheet to the student. Have the student cut out the pictures. Helper reads the clue, and the student says the new word. Then, student finds the picture that matches the new word and glues/tapes or places it in the box next to the sentence *(mow, bat, pet, meal, pig)*.

1. Change the "b" in **bow** to "m" and say the new word.

2. Change the "c" in **cat** to "b" and say the new word.

3. Change the "m" in **met** to "p" and say the new word.

4. Change the "s" in **seal** to "m" and say the new word.

5. Change the "w" in **wig** to "p" and say the new word.

_____ _____ _____
Name                                     Date                                     Helper

 #BK-330 Say & Glue® Phonological Awareness • ©2006 Super Duper® Publications • 1-800-277-8737 • www.superduperinc.com

# Sound Swap

**Directions:** Cut along the dotted line and give the bottom sheet to the student. Have the student cut out the pictures. Helper reads the clue, and the student says the new word. Then, student finds the picture that matches the new word and glues/tapes or places it in the box next to the sentence *(kid, dog, bell, pan, mat)*.

1. Change the "l" in **lid** to "k" and say the new word.

2. Change the "h" in **hog** to "d" and say the new word.

3. Change the "w" in **well** to "b" and say the new word.

4. Change the "t" in **tan** to "p" and say the new word.

5. Change the "s" in **sat** to "m" and say the new word.

_____     _____     _____
Name                                          Date                                       Helper

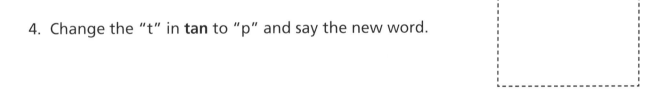

# Sound Substitution

**Directions:** Cut along the dotted line and give the bottom sheet to the student. Have the student cut out the pictures. Helper reads the clue, and the student says the new word. Then, student finds the picture that matches the new word and glues/tapes or places it in the box next to the sentence (*lip, book, cat, ape, ham*).

1. Change the "t" in **lit** to "p" and say the new word.

2. Change the "t" in **boot** to "k" and say the new word.

3. Change the "p" in **cap** to "t" and say the new word.

4. Change the "t" in **ate** to "p" and say the new word.

5. Change the "d" in **had** to "m" and say the new word.

Name          Date          Helper

#BK-330 Say & Glue® Phonological Awareness • ©2006 Super Duper® Publications • 1-800-277-8737 • www.superduperinc.com

# Word Wonders

**Directions:** Cut along the dotted line and give the bottom sheet to the student. Have the student cut out the pictures. Helper reads the clue, and the student says the new word. Then, student finds the picture that matches the new word and glues/tapes or places it in the box next to the sentence *(meat, rope, sit, cap, ram)*.

1. Change the "l" in **meal** to "t" and say the new word.

2. Change the "s" in **rose** to "p" and say the new word.

3. Change the "p" in **sip** to "t" and say the new word.

4. Change the "t" in **cat** to "p" and say the new word.

5. Change the "t" in **rat** to "m" and say the new word.

_____     _____     _____
Name                Date                Helper

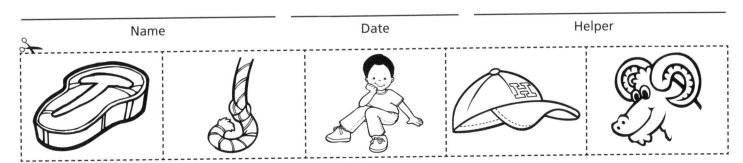

# Sound Switch

**Directions:** Cut along the dotted line and give the bottom sheet to the student. Have student cut out the pictures. Helper reads the clue, and the student says the new word. Then, student finds the picture that matches the new word and glues/tapes or places it in the box next to the sentence *(clock, bike, cup, crib, ship)*.

1. Change the "ĭ" in **click** to "ŏ" and say the new word.

2. Change the "ā" in **bake** to "ī" and say the new word.

3. Change the "ă" in **cap** to "ŭ" and say the new word.

4. Change the "ă" in **crab** to "ĭ" and say the new word.

5. Change the "ŏ" in **shop** to "ĭ" and say the new word.

Name       Date       Helper

   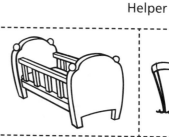 

 #BK-330 Say & Glue® Phonological Awareness • ©2006 Super Duper® Publications • 1-800-277-8737 • www.superduperinc.com

# Mysterious Manipulation

**Directions:** Cut along the dotted line and give the bottom sheet to the student. Have the student cut out the pictures. Helper reads the clue, and the student says the new word. Then, student finds the picture that matches the new word and glues/tapes or places it in the box next to the sentence *(bed, cab, bag, sick, rock)*.

1. Change the "ĭ" in **bid** to "ĕ" and say the new word.

2. Change the "ŭ" in **cub** to "ă" and say the new word.

3. Change the "ĭ" in **big** to "ă" and say the new word.

4. Change the "ă" in **sack** to "ĭ" and say the new word.

5. Change the "ă" in **rack** to "ŏ" and say the new word.

_____  _____  _____
Name                                          Date                                          Helper

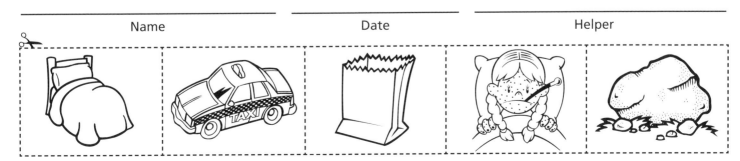

# Marvelous Manipulation

**Directions:** Cut along the dotted line and give the bottom sheet to the student.  Have the student cut out the pictures.  Helper reads the clue, and the student says the new word.  Then, student finds the picture that matches the new word and glues/tapes or places it in the box next to the sentence *(sock, cheese, cob, rag, truck)*.

1.  Change the "ĭ" in **sick** to "ŏ" and say the new word.

2.  Change the "o͞o" in **choose** to "e͞e" and say the new word.

3.  Change the "ă" in **cab** to "ŏ" and say the new word.

4.  Change the "ŭ" in **rug** to "ă" and say the new word.

5.  Change the "ă" in **track** to "ŭ" and say the new word.

_____       _____       _____
Name                                            Date                                            Helper

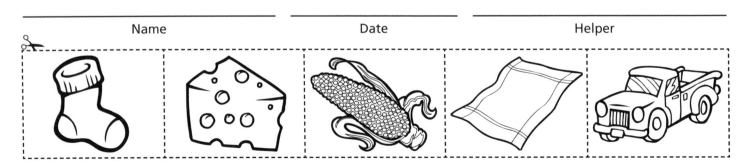

 Manipulation of Phonemes        #BK-330  Say & Glue® Phonological Awareness  •  ©2006 Super Duper® Publications  •  1-800-277-8737  •  www.superduperinc.com

_____ **has made**

**Name**

# phenomenal strides in
# phonological awareness!

_____

**Teacher**

_____

**Date**

---

_____

**Name**

# is a
# Radical Rhymer!

_____                    _____

**Teacher**                                                          **Date**

*This award for beautiful blending of words goes to...*

_____
**Name**

_____               _____
**Teacher**                              **Date**

---

# You Really Caught On to Sound Segmenting!

_____
**Name**

_____               _____
**Teacher**                              **Date**

---

_____
**Name**

## *You're Smashing at Syllable Counting!*

_____               _____
**Teacher**                              **Date**

#BK-330 Say & Glue® Phonological Awareness • ©2006 Super Duper® Publications • 1-800-277-8737 • www.superduperinc.com

# You're a Sound Identification Super Sleuth!

_____
**Name**

_____    _____
**Teacher**    **Date**

---

# You caught the wave of deleting syllables!

_____
**Name**

_____    _____
**Teacher**    **Date**

---

# YOUR SOUND DELETING SKILLS ARE OUT OF THIS WORLD!

**Name** _____

**Teacher** _____

**Date** _____

# YOU'RE AN ACE AT WORD BUILDING!

Name _____

Teacher _____

Date _____

---

# You are a Super Sound Swapper!

_____
**Name**

_____        _____
**Teacher**                                    **Date**

---

# Read All About It!

_____
**Name**

# Has Done Great Work

_____        _____
**Teacher**                                    **Date**

#BK-330 Say & Glue® Phonological Awareness • ©2006 Super Duper® Publications • 1-800-277-8737 • www.superduperinc.com